'A real blast! A woman traveller from India conquers the world like nobody has done since the days of Columbus, but hers is a spiritual conquest—spanning the gamut from ancient Asian temple culture to New World new-ageism, through heart-warming solo trips for the soul. Perhaps, the most motivational travel read since the *Lonely Planet* was invented.'

—Zac O'Yeah
Author of *A Walk Through Barygaza* and *Digesting India*

By the same Author

Table for One
A Solo Living Manual for the Curious Indian Woman

The Inner Light
A Beginner's Guide to Spirituality and Finding Peace

The Monks Who Laughed When the Bumblebee Stung Me

Discovering the Self through Chance Encounters

SUMAA TEKUR

Hay House Publishers India
New Delhi • London • Sydney
Carlsbad, California • New York City

Hay House Publishers (India) Pvt. Ltd.
Muskaan Complex, Plot No.3, B-2 Vasant Kunj, New Delhi-110 070, India
Hay House Inc., PO Box 5100, Carlsbad, CA 92018-5100, USA
Hay House UK, Ltd., The Sixth Floor, Watson House, 54 Baker Street, W1U 7BU, UK
Hay House Australia Pty Ltd., 18/36 Ralph St., Alexandria NSW 2015, Australia

Email: contact@hayhouse.co.in
www.hayhouse.co.in

ISBN 978-81-19554-08-9
ISBN 978-81-19554-09-6 (ebook)

Printed at Thomson Press India Ltd

To the eternal free spirit that lies dormant in every woman.

To her, I say: Wake up, walk every inch of this insanely beautiful planet.

Contents

Foreword

The first time I walked into a bar alone, my palms had gone cold with nervousness, and I had the jitters. Despite my best intentions to sit at the bar and enjoy a drink in my own company, I was overwhelmed with fear.

I had watched too many films where the woman's drink was spiked, a stalker found his object of obsession at the bar, and a gunfight broke out with a volley of bullets poking holes in the walls.

My mind toyed with the probability of any of this happening, but then the question remained of what I would sit and do by myself. Those were not the days of the cell phone where I could bury my head in a screen and feign disinterest in my immediate environment. If I ordered a drink and simply sat looking around, just how foolish would I seem!

Right here, at this moment of decision, I had grown by leaps and bounds. My unique spirituality had emerged in the folds of the seemingly insignificant but courageous-to-me decision of going to a bar alone in a foreign country. I had opened the door to adventure, and I expected nothing less than a fascinating exploration.

The tiny bar in the heart of Rome was abuzz with backpackers exchanging travel stories, ordering more beer and pizza, and playing board games. Nervy and under-confident, I took a seat at the bar counter and surveyed the room self-consciously. People were laughing, glugging their pints, and were engaged in intense conversations.

Nobody even cared to look at me, which was a bit of a disappointment.

Feeling more at ease, I quizzed the bartender on the types of beer and then chose a lager. Just as I took my first sip, a tall man leaned over the counter next to me and asked for another round of drinks for his table.

He turned to me and guessing that I was alone, held his hand out, and introduced himself. 'I'm Kevin. Do you want to join us?' he asked. I nodded vigorously and followed him to sit at a table with two American men, an Australian woman, and a Chinese man—all backpacking in Italy.

My first solo bar visit ended with making new friends from around the world, some of whom I am still in touch with. Thank you, Facebook. But this was possible only because I took that first step into the unknown. Solo travel has been largely about that first step for me. Each time, every time.

I started travelling solo first by dint of circumstance and then increasingly by conscious choice. The Indian culture doesn't typically promote self-exploration by travelling out into the world. If anything, an inner exploration through spirituality is encouraged.

Solo travel clashes with the culture's inherent belief of how to find oneself. It is socially acceptable—desirable even—to find oneself through, say, religion in a social setting. But solo travel? If at all, solo travel is seen at best as a distraction from community-centric values, a brief timeout from the family focus.

Stereotypes abound on why a woman would even want to travel alone. In people's reactions to my lone ranger adventures, I encountered many outdated stereotypes—I must be mending a broken heart; I must be a loner; I must have bad social skills that no one would like to travel with me; or, get this, I must be looking for love.

When we think of a woman travelling solo, we rarely uphold her desire to explore the world, expand her knowledge, and immerse in cultural experiences while enjoying her time alone, independent of her relationship status or social life.

For centuries, women were denied the freedom to roam freely outside of their homes and minds. So, they turned inward and amplified their emotions, making how they feel everything because they lived in their mind most of the time.

As a society, we believe a woman does not need to be alone. It is as though she has no need to think independently, to be assertive, to discover her identity as a woman, and to be self-standing—not in relation to a man or to her relationships. She was certainly not allowed, let alone encouraged, to explore the world unchaperoned or without a man who was a legally sanctioned companion, husband, father, or son.

Women have grown to fear stepping outside because of the physical and moral risk it poses. 'Could I be molested in this neighbourhood?' 'They are going to question my motive for traveling to the hills without a husband or son.'

Culturally, the female dress kept women bound to the home. The metal bindings used in corsets were called 'stays'. These ensured that the woman always needed help in dressing and un-dressing. In the Oriental cultures, women had to bind their feet, which restricted their movement. The 'stays' and 'feet binding' emerged from the historical perspectives of female beauty that women themselves were not consulted on but was enforced on them as a norm for social acceptance.

It took women centuries to free their bodies, but it is taking even longer to free our minds.

Although this gender imbalance is true for every part of the world, these social perceptions are truer for India when compared to most Western cultures. Being Indian sometimes put me at a rare advantage in that the people I met were so curious to hear my story that they voluntarily shared their own fascinating life stories during my journeys. In that, my presence and my ethnicity became my greatest strengths, not weaknesses.

Solo travel is not something that I instantly grew to love. It is an acquired taste that snuck up on me after I had indulged it long enough. There were unpleasant experiences, too, as with any travel. But I found value in it early on and persisted, eventually towards attaining a rewarding transformational world view.

I experienced the human spirit's most enduring qualities—compassion, courage, and hope—cut across borders, language, and culture. In my travel notes, I had subconsciously chronicled a part of my own spiritual journey.

Solo travel tested my courage and relationship with the self. Going solo didn't necessarily mean that I had to do everything on my own. I had the kindness of many strangers along the way to open doors of possibilities. I learned to accept help. I sharpened my intuition and my observation skills. This book is also about how these experiences kindled a deeper understanding of people and cultures.

This book is not a checklist for aspiring solo travellers. It is not a guide; it is not where you'll find itineraries. It doesn't tell travellers what to do, what not to do, where to go, where not to go. Every traveller will make that choice for herself. This book reveals the choices I made, and the outcome of my choices. I tell the stories of how being on the road, alone, changed me.

Wherever I go in the world, I carry the old-fashioned journalist in me that prefers long-form literature, asks questions endlessly, carries a ceaseless curiosity and comes away with an expanded mind.

In writing this book, I gave myself permission to be vulnerable, to lower my guard and potter about in the deep recesses of my mind, bringing those thoughts to paper. In that sense, this book is as much an inner journey as it is about exploring our lonely planet. It is about how travel informed my personal spirituality, influenced it, and paved the path for well-rounded spiritual connections—with people, places, and with Mother Earth.

I MEET

These encounters with strangers expanded my world view, opening doors to fresh ways of thinking, feeling, and healing. Some special encounters, however brief, have the power to forever change our lives. And to meet these people, we cross the seas and undertake great journeys of the land and mind.

1

Desi Ghetto in Barcelona Pulsates with Shared History

I stood at the edge of La Rambla street in the heart of Barcelona, willing my trusty intuition to guide me once again. Should I follow a stranger who beckoned me into the back alleys or hang back in the comforting anonymity of the crowd? Stories tempted me from the hidden alleys, tugging at my curiosity.

On La Rambla, Barcelona's showpiece street, the space was manicured for tourist delight. La Rambla is known to be the liveliest and most colourful single street in Barcelona, filled with shopping and street performers.

Bright lights, restaurants and street artistes amused the jaywalkers strolling casually, taking in the sensory overload in a foreign city. But the hidden is always more enticing. I asked my inner voice: Was this man to be trusted? I wrestled with the conflict as Shahzaad Anjam urged me to follow him to his part of the city.

Only thirty minutes earlier, I had arrived in Barcelona on a weekend trip from London. I was enchanted by everything that I had read about this stylish Spanish city, particularly about Antoni Gaudi's architecture—I wanted to see, touch, and feel the beauty of his creations.

As I walked towards the bus stop, looking uncertainly at the long line of parked buses, I spotted Anjam sucking on the last bit of his cigarette. Tall, slim, and with a tanned and wrinkled face, he wore a dark-coloured pinstriped shirt. He had facial features that made him seem Indian. He was staring at me, perhaps waiting for me to approach him for directions. Warily, I asked him how to get to La Rambla, the tree-lined central street in Barcelona. He gestured to follow him.

In the short, three-minute walk to the bus stop, we struck up an awkward conversation. It started with him asking: 'Indian?'

I nodded. 'You?'

'Pakistani,' he said, closely watching my reaction from the corner of his eye. I didn't bat an eyelid even though my heart may have skipped a beat.

'Vacation?' he asked again, in his mixed accent that drawled heavily around the vowels.

'Yes. I am here from London for the weekend,' I offered some information.

'You have hotel booking?'

I nodded, not wanting to share where I would be staying, and quickly changed the subject, asking him how long it would take me to reach La Rambla.

'Thirty minutes. It's very close by,' he said.

He then pointed towards the bus that I should be taking. When I got on the bus and turned around, I saw that he had followed me in. This made me uncomfortable. Only a few minutes earlier, he was standing by the roadside, blowing cigarette smoke in the air aimlessly, and now he wanted to reach the city centre with me. Something seemed off.

As I scrambled for small change in my handbag, Anjam fished out two bus tickets from his pocket and stamped the time on them both—one for me and another for him.

'How much is the ticket?' I demanded to know, still digging for change in my bag. 'It doesn't matter. I had an extra ticket with me, and I used it,' he said.

I protested, but what he said stumped me: 'You are Indian, and I am Pakistani. The politicians may say or do anything. They do lots of things for their own benefit. But we are brothers and sisters.'

Of all places, I least expected to hear this in Spain's most attractive city. I wanted to trust his words, but my instinctive defence mechanism kicked in and I stepped back, guarded, and cautious.

Anjam may have sensed my caginess. He volunteered information about himself. He told me that although he was born in Pakistan, he likes to think of himself as Spanish. 'You need to adopt the culture of the place you live in,' he said, 'It makes life a lot easier.'

'How long have you been living here?' I asked him, relaxing my guard just a bit.

'Eight years now. I fell in love with a Spanish woman and married her.'

When I asked him what he did for a living, he was evasive. 'Import-export business,' he said, using the common phrase that hustlers use to bypass specific questions about earnings. I double-checked my caution, making a mental note to lose him the minute I got off the bus.

The landscape outside the bus window changed to reveal rows of buildings and fewer trees as we got closer to the city centre. At one stop, Anjam alighted and asked me to follow. He opened his right arm towards the street ahead and declared with a flourish as though presenting a work of art: La Rambla.

I thanked him and said that I was grateful for his help. He wasn't about to let me go just yet. I didn't want him to know where I was staying. So, I played along, hoping to get rid of him soon enough.

Anjam led me to a circular plaza with cobblestones and a giant fountain at the centre called the Fountain of Three Graces. The centrepiece was a sculpture of three women, the three daughters of Zeus, each representing beauty, charm, and joy. I stopped to admire the fountain, which looked spectacular in the bright sunshine and the cloudless sky. I clicked pictures and asked Anjam if I could click his picture. He readily posed.

He then asked me to follow him across the square. I walked along, taking in the sights and sounds of the overcrowded plaza. He stepped into a narrow alleyway that could barely be seen from the main street. I hesitated. I knew I didn't want to be away from the hustle and bustle.

I walked slowly behind Anjam and peeped into the street. I could only see walls, in what looked like a winding alleyway into another neighbourhood. I told Anjam that I needed to go, and decisively wished him good luck and turned to leave. He called out to me and said that he would take me to his neighbourhood for tea.

My heart raced with apprehension but, I also wanted to give in to the suspense. He had let me click his picture. He spoke to me without making me feel threatened. The threat that I felt came from deep down my own guardedness.

Here is where I was checking in for an answer from my intuition. Unlike what most of us believe, an intuitive feeling makes us uncomfortable. It is not a safe haven. At that moment, I experienced discomfort from the lure of a hidden Barcelona tugging at my eternal well of curiosity on the one hand, and on the other, my practical and practised sense of responsibility pulling me behind the walls of safety.

Growing up in India, I was trained—as are most if not all women—to constantly look over my shoulder in public places. I grew up on a steady diet of horror stories that brought to life on screen the pain and suffering caused by being too naïve and too trusting. Caution is woven into the Indian woman's DNA.

In many cases, the excessive sheltering—always having to be in the care of a society-approved male figure, often a father, brother, husband, or son—severely limits the range of experiences open to a woman. These were the limits I was looking to stretch and test with my solo travels. This involved shedding inhibitions, questioning my own conditioning, and making new and brave decisions that were unfamiliar to me.

When a woman travels solo, she takes responsibility for her decisions while weighing the practicality of safe choices on the one hand and giving in to her curiosity on the other. This was a moment when such a decision had to be made.

It was not easy because social conditioning is often so deeply entrenched in our psyche that it is safer to pedal back into our cocoon of comfort while believing that that's all there is to life. We begin to believe that what we are allowed to see is all there is. It is cruel that the burden of her safety falls on the woman alone and is not a shared social responsibility.

The lure of the encounter makes travel enticing. Many times, it is not the encounter itself but the possibility of opening a window to another world, a peep into a life story and a chance to feel empathy for someone from outside our culture. This lure of the encounter brings hope to our hearts.

Anjam watched me expressionless and waited for me to follow him. I took a deep breath and checked in with how I felt at that moment. I had no reason to believe the worst about him. I made a decision to go with the flow. I was only a few steps away from the main street. I wanted to give trust a chance. I wanted to believe that my intuition about this man was not fooling me.

I followed Anjam for a few minutes through the winding alleyway and was shocked to see what opened up before me. I stared wide-eyed and incredulous at what could easily pass off as a middle-class neighbourhood in Mumbai.

'This is St Pau. My house is here,' he said. Anjam and I walked down the desi area of Barcelona.

I saw bay windows; colourful *kameezes* fluttered in the breeze, one end tied to wrought iron balconies; conservatively dressed Asian women pushed prams containing both child and their vegetable shopping. The strong smell of spices, mixed with the floral scent of incense, wafted across the alley. I saw shop fronts sporting photos of Indian gods and goddesses decorated with floral garlands.

These sensory experiences transported me straight back to India. In fact, the scene before me looked more Indian than the typical Indian city today that is seeking to ape the West in look, feel, mood, and style.

Even as urban Indians in India seek to redefine their Indianness through the lens of western influence, modernity, economic development, and success, Indian migrants fervently hold on to pieces of their old life in a foreign cultural setting. They carve out space for their roots, culture, and history as a constant reminder of their identity. I saw proof of this as I walked down the narrow alley in St Pau.

People value one's own culture, food, religion, and social network when in a strange place with unfamiliar etiquette and rules. They miss what they have left behind, but it is in human nature not to let go so easily.

Posters of famous Bollywood stars Aishwarya Rai, Shah Rukh Khan, and Salman Khan adorned the walls of the street full of 'communication centres', a term used loosely to refer to a telephone booth that also operates as a DVD library, internet parlour, mobile accessories store, and watch repair centre. This was 2006, when internet parlours were proliferating, bringing the world ever so closer.

Humans were still getting used to the mobile phone, using the device to primarily make calls and send short text messages. For email, it was still an internet connection, best accessed on a PC at home, or at an internet café that replaced phone booths. These versatile communication centres were run by desis and welcomed all, especially Indians, with a broad smile.

I stopped to speak to a few people. It didn't take much prodding for the desis here to open up about their lives, earnings, or emotional state.

'Cricket and Hindi movies are the common topics of discussion with my Pakistani and Bangladeshi friends, something we don't get to experience in India,' one man from Mumbai said with a wide smile. In this desi land, it is impossible to tell an Indian from a Pakistani.

'For centuries, we have had the same culture. And now, living in a foreign country, we have learnt to celebrate festivals together, dine together and unite in times of need,' said Maqsood Ahmed from Chattarpur in India.

Maqsood had been working as a waiter in La Baguetina restaurant for about a decade. He couldn't rely on his science degree to get him a job in India and crossed the seas in search of a better lifestyle.

He said, 'I invite my Hindu friends to celebrate Eid-ul-Fitr and I go to their houses for Diwali. This is not to say that every time bombs explode in Kashmir, there is no ill feeling.'

'Sparks fly when we discuss Indian-Pakistani politics. But we also have a livelihood to earn and a foreign society to live in. Plus, we know that it is politicians playing tricks and we have nothing against our brothers across the border,' Bangladeshi Adil Singh told me. He laughed and added that Bangladeshis always end up being referees when Indians and Pakistanis play street cricket.

Anjam led me into a chai shop, clearly a favourite in the neighbourhood. The jarring *bhangra* beats from an old cassette-player, the stained white ceramic-tiled walls, and the smell of frying onions that will soon be used as a filling for hot *pakoras* were all sensory surprises, which conflicted with the reality that this was in the heart of Barcelona.

Yet, what made this restaurant conspicuously different from its cousin in Patiala were the Indians, Pakistanis, Bangladeshis, Africans, Koreans, and Spaniards tucking into supple, juicy *rasagullas* and sipping on Indian masala chai, while making small talk in this South Asian neighbourhood in the heart of Barcelona.

More striking was the fact that Indians and Pakistanis shared the same table. Some of the customers were weary travellers and the rest were locals comfortably seated to pass the lazy afternoon at their favourite haunt. For many years, Barcelona had been on my list of cities to visit. It was home to one of the world's most celebrated football clubs. English rock band The Alan Parsons Project's song *La Sagrada Familia* piqued my interest in this eponymous unfinished church, which has been in construction for over 135 years.

And then I had read about Antoni Gaudi's marvels with building design. These are the things I wanted to experience here. But now, in less than an hour of my arrival in this city, I felt like I was back in India, or what India would have been only if some things had taken a different turn in 1947.

'I didn't know that there was such a big Indian community living in Spain,' I told Anjam.

'Scores of desis migrate to Spain because they are able to secure well-paying jobs here and earn a standard of living that is far better than what they can manage back home,' Anjam explained. He said that Spain is the preferred destination because the paperwork for immigration is easier compared to what many other Western countries demand.

Anjam's sister lives in London and his brother is a limousine chauffeur at the White House in Washington. 'I am saving some money to visit my brother in the US so I can become a driver like him. There is more money in that job,' said Anjam, adding that till then, it will be the import-export business for him, and cooking for his beautiful wife, who loves Indian food.

As I interacted with the people from my corner of the world, I momentarily forgot that I was there to experience Gaudi's architecture and see a 'Barcelona' that fit into the experience promised by travel books. I was, instead, drawn into this milieu of people, their activities, and hopes and dreams. I savoured this flavour and let it linger for a while. I asked them more questions about their life and they unhesitatingly answered.

'What do you do in your free time?' I asked at the table of four middle-aged gentlemen, who shared a plate of *rasagullas* with me. 'There are a few temples and mosques that Barcelona's Asian community frequents. There are Sikh gurudwaras also. Sunday visits to holy places have become the norm,' said Anju Singh from Amritsar in India, who overheard our conversation and piped up from another table. She had a thick Punjabi accent.

Living in this foreign country, both Indians and Pakistanis have learnt to put their differences aside. The Line of Control (the military control line in Kashmir which divides India and Pakistan) is no more than a line to citizens from both countries living in this part of the world.

'After all, our eating habits, language, art and culture are similar,' said Ayaz Khan, a shopkeeper in St Pau, summarising the sentiments of the community. I learnt that the degree of cultural tolerance is higher when on foreign soil.

Having enjoyed my cup of tea and plate of samosas at the chai shop, I sat in silence, observing the camaraderie from the mixed communities seated in that tiny restaurant. I heard smatterings of Hindi, Punjabi, and Urdu along with English, and even some Spanish.

Then I snickered at my own apprehensions. I would have missed this entire world within a world if I had given in to my mistrust. This was another win for trust in a world that is growing increasingly dangerous, especially for women who want to live on their own terms.

I smiled at my little personal victory—of letting trust win over fear; of letting my intuition lead the way; and of breaking yet another social-conditioning barrier in my heart.

I waved Anjam goodbye, thanked him, and walked out to the thrill and noise of La Rambla. I found my way to the seaside backpacker hostel, freshened up and walked out to experience Antoni Gaudi's marvellous architecture.

As I stepped out, I wondered why I had to travel all the way to Barcelona to experience India. I got the answer. What I experienced was an undivided India—an India that would have been, only if things were done differently in 1947.

2

Girls' Getaway Forges an Unbreakable Bond by Baikal's Shores

'Govinda.' The restaurant logo was printed in stylish italics of the English alphbet, a rarity in eastern Russia. The dining room was dense and stuffy with heavy brown sofas and elaborate wall murals in neon colours. A giant replica of the Taj Mahal stood against one wall, blinking in psychedelic lights.

This was a self-service restaurant, where you pay for food by weight. I went up to the buffet counter and was greeted by the helper with a bemused expression that said: 'An Indian in an Indian restaurant!'

I chatted him up in my broken Russian, with a lot of help from the translator app, while deciding what to eat. He served one spoon at a time and looked to me through the glass partition for approval to stop or to add more. I had extremely low expectations of the food taste, which it matched. Yet, it was comforting to eat steamed rice and bland curry away from home.

I had plans to visit the art museum on my way back to the hostel. I waved the waiter goodbye and was about to turn when a Russian woman at the counter half-screamed at me, 'Indian! You're from India!' she said, emphasising the yaaa at the end of India.

I smiled, nodded, and turned to leave. 'Come and sit with me,' she ordered, and walked to a table carrying her tray. I stopped in my tracks. That was not a request. It was not a question. It was an order. I was stunned into silence. I was running a quick analysis in my head. If she's this bossy, do I want to sit with her? But then, she speaks English. I haven't spoken to anyone but the hostel receptionist in five days now, another voice in me reasoned.

I could feel it in my gut that this was yet another chance encounter, a serendipitous meeting that travel was offering me. Chances are poetic that way. There is beauty in coincidence. And even though they are all-consuming and powerful, magical even, they give us the opportunity to say no to them.

Here is the thing about chance meetings like these. They synchronistically open up a tantalising world of possibilities, of 'what ifs'. And this is the 'what if' that gets me every single time. Call it, in Gen Z lingo, FOMO (Fear of Missing Out). Every 'what if' carries the mystery of a new morning and a day full of powerful potential.

This Russian woman's offer to sit with her was exactly that. What will I do with the chance this time around?

My thoughts were interrupted by her voice, 'Come here. I'm sitting here,' she waved out to me.

A Russian who speaks English is a treat in Siberia, I told myself, and took the seat opposite her. 'Dina,' she held out her hand by way of introduction. I shook her hand and introduced myself. She asked me all about my travel plans, where I was coming from, where I was headed, and my plans for Irkutsk.

Dina had light green eyes and carried a bouncing mop of black hair that framed her face beautifully. About forty-five years old, I guessed. She was a lawyer, but her real passion was photography, she said. 'I do a spot of photography myself,' I told her.

'Where's your camera?' she asked, half-accusingly, eyes searching. I had gotten accustomed to this brusqueness, a Russian trait. Most Russians don't have the patience for politeness, which they take for being fake. Politeness is for the ones who have a lot of time on hand, they believe. Brusqueness aside, Dina was one of the most large-hearted friends I made in the entire month I spent travelling across the biggest country in the world.

Dina spoke of her Indian connection. 'I have visited India twice. My soul belongs there,' she said in a soft tone, a faraway look in her eyes. Her eyes moistened. 'How did you like the food here?' she asked abruptly, shaking me out of thoughts of my home country.

'It was okay,' I shrugged, non-committal.

'It's rubbish,' she said, as she tucked into a mouthful of chickpea salad, mixed with tomato salsa.

'What's your plan for this evening?' she asked.

'I plan to visit the art museum,' I said, taking that it was the cue to part ways.

'Forget museum. Let's go to Lake Baikal,' she said. Again, it was a decision. She wasn't asking me. She was telling me.

'But I am going there tomorrow anyway,' I said by way of explanation, completely confused and a bit wary as to why she wanted to drive 65 km one way, when it was past 5 p.m.

'So what? You can go again. But you can go today also,' she said, having already made up her mind.

We talked about this for a few more minutes. I was explaining the wastefulness of making a double trip to the same place. But Dina had already made the decision. A few moments later, I realised that this was about her, not me. She wanted to click pictures of the lake, hoping to get some beautiful sunset shots.

It was decided. We both first walked to my hostel, where I picked up my camera. We then took a taxi to her house where she changed from her work clothes, fed her two cats—Salvador Dali and Frida Kahlo—and picked up her camera.

As I sat in her living room, sipping Siberian special tea made from brusnika wild red berries, her cats staring at me, visibly unhappy with my presence, I thought about how easily I trusted this woman whom I met only an hour ago. And now we were going on a road trip. The truth is that somewhere in her eyes, not too deep, I had spotted loneliness. It was the yearning for female companionship, a sisterhood that she probably missed. Loneliness is that constant which cuts across class, gender, caste, geography, and education. It is what forms some of the most mismatched but lasting connections.

I had, not for the first time, gone against every precocious urge to hold back and protect my space. There is something about travel that dismisses logic and heightens intuition, the shorter route to decision-making. Little did I know that one decision to lean in to the tantalising 'what if' would lead to an enduring friendship that would transcend the seas and go strong for several years and still counting.

Dina drove fast. Very fast. I commented about the speed and she said that it is the way Russians are. She cautioned me against crossing the road without a pedestrian crossing sign. 'This is not Indiyaaa,' she mock-laughed. Russian car drivers will run over you and not flinch for a second, she said.

I again asked her about the decision to drive to the lake. She became thoughtful and revealed that Lake Baikal invigorates her, and that she feels healed, blessed, and beautiful to be around this biggest freshwater lake in the world. As we drove past the Taiga Forest, she shared factual titbits about the lake.

'It is the deepest lake in the world. Its biodiversity is much like sea life, but it is actually a freshwater lake. It is a mystery for scientists the world over.'

But more interestingly for Dina, it is how she feels around the lake that makes her want to go back there again and again.

'You're going to Olkhon Island, right? There's a shaman rock there called Burkhan, which is powerful and healing. The Siberian shamans lived around the lake and drew energy from it, working with this powerful force of nature,' she said, talking softly in a tone that exuded faith, deep respect, and devotion.

'I'm always ready to go to Lake Baikal,' she suddenly cheered up and smiled, explaining to me again the reason for the spontaneous trip. Here was her feeble attempt at masking her loneliness. She was proactively converting what would perhaps be a noiseless evening with her cats in her sombre apartment, into a road trip with a new friend from a country she loves.

The first glimpse of Lake Baikal, to my right, was breathtaking. I first drew in a sharp breath at this wonderful sight and then I let out a sigh at the vastness of this lake. It was unlike anything I had ever seen—a large water body that was ostensibly calm. It had none of the wildness of ocean waves, nor did it have the rumble of hitting the shore with a powerful slap and sweep every few seconds. I thought I heard, instead, a gentle hum that comes from stillness and wisdom. There was a sparkle to the lake's presence, slivers of silver shimmering and dancing on its surface.

The clouds played hide-and-seek with the sun, alternately changing the colour of the water. It was sometimes dark grey, sometimes green, and sometimes blue. It was as though the lake didn't want to be understood, or that it was simply impossible to pin her down.

As though reading my mind, Dina said: 'Don't take the lake's calmness for granted. When she gets angry, she creates havoc. Read about the Sarma wind,' she said, teasing me to ask her more. So, I asked.

'Sarma is a terrible wind that blows from the mountain gorge at Olkhon Island. It destroys everything that comes in its way. When it is angry, it comes like a hurricane and entire houses also fly away.' I stared at the lake trying to picture this vast open and deep water body capable of such violent destruction.

It must be special that I saw the lake for the first time with Dina, who feels so passionately about it. She stopped the car at a height from where the lake spread out splendidly far below. For mid-May, the start of summer in Siberia, the air was bitingly cold, needing me to wear my gloves and hat.

Dina took her camera from the backseat and beckoned me to follow. I thought she was walking ahead to get a better view. Instead, she started to trek down the rocks to get closer to the water. I wasn't sure that was a good idea. There was not a soul in sight, and the hill was steep. 'Are you sure?' I shouted. She just waved in my direction to follow her. So, follow I did.

A fifteen-minute moderately difficult trek down the slippery rocks, during which I feared more for my camera than my body, we reached the water. I dipped my hands for the first time in the water, which was cold to the touch. And yet, I felt a warm shiver of emotion. A current of powerful energy hit me. It was a mix of compassion, warmth, and calm.

As I walked along the rocky shore of Lake Baikal, my attention was drawn to an aquamarine piece of glass. Broken off a bottle, it was lying at the water's edge. The repeated flow of water over this piece had smoothed its sharp edges.

It showed me how water, a seemingly gentle element of nature, could tame the sharpness of glass through quiet persistence over time. I kept that piece of glass with me as a reminder of nature's wonder.

The clouds were changing formation as Dina and I tried to capture the sun setting behind the beauty of Baikal. We clicked away for a long time in silence, in the comforting companionship of artists tending to their craft. Dina clicked my first portraits against the stunning beauty of Lake Baikal, a prized possession that made for impressive professional-quality pictures. Then I clicked hers. We took the mandatory selfies.

When the light started to fade, we drove back. My eyelids grew heavy from the weight of jetlag and travel fatigue, but I kept up the conversation till Dina dropped me off at the hostel. She promised to meet me upon my return to Irkutsk two days later. And she did.

This time she carried her best warm clothes, winter boots, and new sets of thermals, woollen socks, sweaters, and the warmest jacket. She unloaded all these clothes from her bag on to my bed, and explained: 'You're from India. You have no idea how punishing Siberian cold can be. You're going to Olkhon Island tomorrow and I have checked the weather report. It is going to be cold, windy, and rainy. You'll need all of these. And wear these shoes. They wil keep you warm.'

She had even packed a bottle of brusnika berries, which I just needed to mix into hot water and drink, to keep warm and build immunity from the cold.

Here, unexpectedly from a random restaurant visit, I had found a friend, a sister from another lifetime, who shared warmth and humanity. It was after meeting Dina, again, that I understood the power of serendipity. Chance encounters can indeed be a life-changing force of such magnitude that they can breathe life into a most mundane daily occurrence.

The power of serendipity allows us to deeply reflect on our existence and what chance meetings signal to us. For me, the meeting with Dina signalled the need to trust my intuition, to be spontaneous, and to surrender to the moment that promised an experience that no amount of planning or prepping could ever offer.

The chance meeting was bringing me to the present, away from the past of what I hoped for that moment, and also away from the future of what I wanted the next few moments to be. I read somewhere that serendipity is more potent than fate. Fate has a ring of finality to it. But serendipity? It is full of possibility. Therein lies its beauty.

If we could see serendipity, I would imagine us all as colourful balls of cosmic light colliding with each other, by lucky chance, and making a unique mix of colours from the collision. How wonderful that would be!

Chance cannot be explained. And that which cannot be explained earns a mystical aura. I see my chance meetings through my travels in this otherworldly light. There is a reason why they happen. But the beauty is mostly in the agency of our decision to submit to the 'what if' or move away.

For the next four meetings till I had Irkutsk as my base for travel around Lake Baikal, I kept meeting Dina. She took me to another Indian restaurant, Ganga, in the city.

She led me to her favourite place to get the best view of the city. It was on top of an abandoned water tank. We climbed up the creaky steps to take stunning sunset photos. She brought local spices for me to carry. She gave me food that would last me many train rides. We drank a lot of tea together, laughed a lot, and shared many stories in the brief moments that we could steal.

Through my trip to Russia, Dina stayed in contact, ever ready to help when I needed anything at all. Sometimes, I would click pictures of signboards I didn't understand, and she would translate them for me.

When an old Russian woman treated me badly and I felt awful, she reprimanded me for being oversensitive. She shared her perspective on relationships. Although cynical after quitting two marriages, Dina was strong, refusing to fall for the trap of self-sabotage.

Dina is the first friend I made in Russia. We made plans to travel together in the not-so-distant future. Dina showed me that chance encounters have the power to be life-transforming and life-affirming.

Her friendship made me want to travel more for travel's sake, for a vibrant criss-cross of cultural exchange. Travel has the power to shed the walls we erect to lock ourselves in, in the name of keeping people out. How wonderful it would be to raze those walls. 'Countries without borders,' as Dina said.

3

Bamboo Train in Battambang Makes a Stop at Childhood Central

I made a day's stop at Battambang while travelling through Cambodia for a silly but absolutely delightful reason: The bamboo train. My inner child was clapping and hopping in glee at the thought of riding an open-air, makeshift train called Norry. What was even better was that the ride would be with no purpose other than to, well, go on a ride.

I reached Battambang in the evening from Siem Reap by local bus. After checking in to a hotel, I walked the deserted roads to the market area and chose a restaurant for dinner. A group of loud, elderly men were having a rollicking time over beer and jokes at the restaurant's longest centre table. I was the only other customer.

The chocolate-coloured plastic tables and chairs were clean but not much thought had gone into matching more than their colour. When I sat, I sunk so low in the chair that the table almost came up to my nose.

I had arranged to meet Thean, a travel guide-cum-tuk-tuk driver, on a friend's recommendation. Tuk-tuk, for the uninitiated, is a carriage drawn by a motorcycle. The carriage seats five persons, has a roof, and is open on the sides. I used the restaurant's Wi-Fi to inform him of my whereabouts. He arrived within five minutes as I took the second sip of my cold beer.

'I have all day tomorrow before I hop on the night bus further south to Sihanoukville,' I told him. 'I prefer to take the off-the-beaten track and see the unusual sights rather than the touristy places,' I emphasised.

Thean seemed to understand. He gave me the plan. 'We will start with the bamboo train ride. Then I will take you to a few ancient temple ruins. And then we will visit the killing caves. Then I will take you up a hill to see the mountaintop view. From there, you will see the bat caves,' he said, giving me a rehearsed version of the same itinerary that he sells to all his tourist-clients.

'Everything sounds great. Could you also take me to the surrounding villages? I would like to see authentic Cambodian village life,' I said. He nodded, and we agreed to meet at 9 a.m. the following morning.

At 8:15 the next morning, I walked down the stairs from my room to the reception. 'Your tuk-tuk driver is here,' said the receptionist. I wondered why he was there so early when I had said 9 a.m. He seemed a little on the heavier side and darker-skinned this morning. But then I saw him last night in the poor restaurant lighting, I thought to myself.

I caught his eye and then pointed to my watch to indicate that there was still time to start the tour. He didn't seem to be in a hurry. I told him that I have not had breakfast yet.

'I'll take you,' he said. I was going to eat at the restaurant opposite the hotel, but he led me to one a few buildings away. 'This is better,' he said. It was indeed better. It was where the locals ate authentic Cambodian noodle soup. There was also toast and tea. He sat across me from the table but didn't talk. I didn't either. It was still too early in the morning. I needed to sit in silence.

My morning tea, toast, and a fruit later, I felt energetic and ready to take on the day. With a sprightly spring in my step, I got chatty with Thean. He struggled to keep up with my English. I found this odd, too, compared to the previous evening when he seemed more confident.

I wanted to finalise the tuk-tuk rental for the day. We haggled with each other and arrived at a price that was more in his favour than mine. With that out of the way, I was ready for my joyride. My inner child yelped in glee.

We set off to O Dambong for the bamboo train ride, the highlight of Battambang, and the sole reason I made the road trip to this north-western part of the country. It was a thirty-minute ride outside the city, crossing fields and villages to reach the entrance to a railway station.

It had to be the smallest train station in the world. Thean waited at the tuk-tuk parking while I went inside the station. There were a few other tourists, all Caucasians. It was not difficult to navigate the ticket purchase. Everyone knows why you're there. A local approached me and asked for $5 for a return ride that I would be sharing with a young male backpacker. I paid up and waited for my 'train'.

A three-meter square sheet made of bamboo slats was set on barbell-like bogies. This was connected through a belt to a small diesel-run motorcycle engine. A straw mat and cushions were laid on top of the bamboo sheet. I sat cross-legged on a cushion with much trepidation. When our 'driver' pulled the manual starter, the engine whirred to life. The bamboo train rolled on the tracks, first slowly and then picked up speed of about 40 kmph.

The tracks were less than smooth, making the ride rickety at best and risky at worst. There was nothing to hold on to but my sense of adventure. There were no seatbelts, no announcements, and no safety guidelines. The train had no regard for safety and let you roll down the train tracks on a sheet of bamboo. No serious accidents or irreparable injuries have ever been reported from these tracks. Tourists flocked to Battambang just for this experience. It was dangerous, fast, and foolish.

I embraced the openness and rode close to nature, often coming within inches of shrubs, bushes, and trees. This was the entire thrill of the ride.

The sun was beating down but as the train rattled across fields, bridges, brooks, and tiny villages, the cool air engulfed me, making the ride a visual and sensual delight. A bed of green unfolded all around me and I was trundling alongside trees, bushes, and streams of fresh water. I felt a whoop of joy.

A childhood fantasy came true. This was even better than the toy trains; it had no windows or doors and nothing to obstruct the view, I felt one with nature. I looked up at the sky and inhaled the scent of freedom.

The train gradually slowed down and I saw another train on the opposite side. The rule was that the train with more passengers got right of way. It had four tourists while mine had just two. So, I hopped off the bamboo sheet and the train was disassembled. First, the driver took off the cushions and the straw mat, then off came the sheet. The barbells were placed on the side and the engine was lifted away from the tracks to make way for the other train. The train was then assembled together in seconds and we rode on.

The seven-km twenty-minute ride from O Dombong to O Sra Lav was a journey without purpose. Upon reaching the village of O Sra Lav, the driver took a ten-minute break. This was mostly to allow the villagers to sell food and souvenirs to tourists. Every tourist was told to tip the driver.

I knew what to expect on the ride back to O Dombong. I sat comfortably, breathed easy and lived the moment for its simplicity, innovation, and joie de vivre. Movement had never felt so carefree, so light.

This uniquely liberating experience was the bang for my buck (five bucks, actually); it was the win to my bet on Battambang. It was an aimless, silly ride. But how I loved it!

Even though I intended to go on this ride and had planned to travel across the country for just this, during those carefree moments on the norry, I encountered the joy of spontaneity. Nothing could prepare me for the unfiltered freedom of zooming at top speed on that open-air ride.

We are used to living in a world of safety and regulation. In such strictly structured formats of being, the joy of breaking the rules and living with a bit of adventure is a delicious one. I will always cherish the innocent experience from this norry ride. It reminded me what it could be like to knock on unknown doors and to explore the zillion pathways we could be walking, all with the promise of different sceneries and scenarios. With travel, although we seek out the joy of a change of scene, what we actually desire is to meet a different part of ourselves.

On that norry ride, with my hair wildly dancing in the wind and my desire to scream at the top of my lungs, I had met my carefree self. It had felt stuck, buried beneath years of 'should' and 'must'.

Here, I was meeting that buoyant emotion again only to realise that both freedom and restriction are what I make it out to be. They were both within me at all times, at a comfortable distance for me to reach when I desired, and for them to disappear when I desired so. In that sense, freedom and restriction are illusory, I realised.

It was during this moment when my inhibitions were cut loose that I experienced total self-acceptance. The past or the future did not matter. What I felt at the very moment was the only thing that mattered. I was meeting my true self, where I didn't feel inadequate, nor did I feel haughty. I just felt present to that moment in time.

Sometimes, when working at my desk, a faint gush of wind is all it takes to whisk me away to another place and time. I dream of being elsewhere, doing something else. The bamboo train, with its unabashed delivery of adventure, was doing the opposite by bringing me back to the here and now. There was nowhere else I wanted to be.

On this silly train ride, I had had a profound spiritual encounter with the Self. Time didn't stand still. Time just didn't matter because I was fully aware and present to that experience. The joy of spontaneity is that it could turn out either messy or lovely, or both. The bamboo train ride was beyond these descriptions. It simply was the purest version of itself.

Thean flashed a wide grin when he saw that I looked so pleased. He kickstarted the tuk-tuk and off we went to explore more of Battambang. After a short distance riding on the highway, Thean swerved off the main road onto a narrow, winding village road. Riding deep into the paddy fields, I saw tiny houses and local life with villagers shopping for vegetables, sweeping the front yard, watering plants, and playing with children. We then turned away from the main road on to a dirt track.

'Are we going to see the ancient temples you spoke of yesterday?' I asked above the sound of the tuk-tuk.

'We're going into the village. I'm showing you Cambodian village life,' the driver shouted back. I found this both odd and interesting. Why hadn't he mentioned this plan to me yesterday?

The bamboo train ride had set the tone for what was to be one of the most fascinating cultural experiences of my travelling life. We first stopped at a house where I saw the making of massive cement pots. Designed to resemble a giant urn at least four feet tall and three feet wide, I saw how they used wooden slats to shape these pots and allow the cement to set before removing the slats.

These large water tanks are now mostly used for commercial water storage in a country where water is a scarce resource. Rural Cambodians predominantly store water in cement tanks rather than plastic ones. But this, like many other local industries, is dying in the face of rapid westernisation, Thean explained.

We then rode further inside the village to stop before a makeshift shed in which an aged woman was charcoal-grilling sticky rice in bamboo. The dish is called Kralan or Khao Lam. Rice soaked overnight in water is stuffed along with red beans, sugar, and shaved coconut inside the cavity of a six-inch bamboo stick. This is then grilled over hot charcoal for ten minutes, turning it around frequently for even heat distribution. When ready, you peel the bamboo and eat the rice, which gets an earthy, raw, and rich flavour.

'This is all really good. Why didn't you tell me about all this yesterday?' I asked Thean, more out of curiosity than accusation. He simply smiled and looked away. We rode out of the village and back on to the highway to enter a fish market. The smells and sights were unpleasant with much blood and gore. So, I asked Thean to keep going and not stop.

Along the way, we crossed several houses. By the entrance to each house, I saw a tower, at least five feet tall. It was decorated in ethnic design and colours. It looked like a treehouse. But Thean said that it was a spirit house. Every house in Cambodia would keep one.

'We always keep food and drink in the spirit house,' he said, explaining that any passing spirits, even ancestors that may want to enter the house, are respectfully asked to partake of food and water from the spirit house and bless the land with calm and peace. This is done mostly to prevent paranormal activity or unhappy ancestors and passing spirits.

We then stopped at a local rice-wine factory, where Thean urged me to taste snake wine. He had scooped a ladle of translucent liquid from a glass jar at the bottom of which rested a dead snake.

'It is strong snake wine. We drink it like medicine here,' he urged me to drink up.

I took the shot of snake wine in one quick gulp. Tasting like spiced liquid, it burned my insides with its pungency. Snake wine usually has a venomous snake infused in the jar of alcoholic rice wine. In Southeast Asian countries, it is popularly believed to cure every known ailment from migraines and vision impairments to asthma and skin disease. The taste was so strong that I could not have another round.

The next stop was a rice-sheet factory, where I saw the handmade production of spring roll sheets. I had witnessed such a fascinating array of cottage industries in rural Cambodia, all surprises that I hadn't expected from this town.

It was well past 2 p.m. but I wasn't bored for a second. We stopped for lunch at a local eatery for rice and steamed vegetables. Post this brief break, we proceeded to the thirty-minute ride outside the city to Phnom Sampeou, a pagoda atop a hillock with beautiful views across Battambang.

The pagoda itself was similar to the other Buddhist temples I had visited in the region. But the views were worth the ride up. I walked back slowly and waited by a café for the event of the evening—the spectacle from the bat caves. I ordered lemonade and sat on a plastic chair waiting with a motley bunch of tourists, again mostly Caucasians.

At exactly 5:45 p.m. the bats started to fly out of a cave on the side of the mountain. They came in hundreds, and thousands and then millions. They were disciplined and snaked their way out of the caves to the far horizon.

This incredible show of nature lasted over thirty minutes. The bats flew out in large numbers into the natural surroundings, perhaps, for a night of hunting. Once the twilit-sky was clear of the bats, the crowds climbed into their respective tuk-tuks and within minutes disappeared into the horizon.

On my forty-five-minute ride back to the hotel, as I reflected on the eventful, wholesome, and adventurous day, little did I know that the twist in the tale had yet to come. We reached the hotel and I profusely thanked Thean for taking me around town so willingly, and for perfectly understanding my need to go off the beaten track.

I paid him for the day's tuk-tuk rental with a generous tip. He gave me his card. The name on his card mentioned his name as Ola. I was confused.

'You're Ola? What about Thean? Is it your nickname?' I asked. He shook his head, pretending to not hear and quickly started his tuk-tuk to be on his way.

Still confused, I walked into the hotel reception. I heard a loud 'Hello!' behind me. Seated on the sofa was a man who looked very similar to the man I had met the previous evening at the restaurant.

'Where did you go? I wait for you all day,' he said, visibly upset.

I felt the ground beneath my feet give way. I had gone on the day's excursion with another tuk-tuk driver and not with the one I had promised! I stood staring ahead of me for two full minutes at Thean, my mouth open in disbelief. Was he lying? Or had I been such a fool?

When I regained my composure, I apologised to Thean and tried to explain that I thought I went with him because they looked alike. It was such a feeble and flimsy argument. So, I stopped trying to explain. I only kept apologising. Thean then shrugged and left.

I asked the young lady at the reception if he waited all day. She nodded. I felt terrible and didn't know how to repair this. The truth is that I couldn't repair it. It was meant to be this way, and I had to accept it.

Being conned is not a pleasant feeling at all. It hits at the heart of trust. I began to question the good day of travel that I had just experienced. All of those experiences now seemed tainted with this one episode of impersonation. I was caught in the crossfire of two tuk-tuk drivers who were vying for my business.

For Ola, impersonating Thean was a simple matter of earning for the day. For Thean, the day-long wait was a matter of a broken promise. For me, the false information and cheating had broken my trust.

When I tried to read this situation through philosophical lenses, I could glean a larger purpose to this incident, something that was perhaps important to complete certain 'transactions' and clear some karmic dues.

Perhaps, I was meant to drink snake wine and visit the old lady selling sticky bamboo rice. And perhaps, it was Ola's karmic duty to show me all those places. No meeting is accidental or without purpose, I believe, and so it is with my encounters with Thean and Ola.

I felt angry and cheated. But the more emotional distance I got from this incident, the more I was capable of finding the humour in it. It is now one of my most favourite travel stories.

A few months later when a friend planned to visit Cambodia, I gave him the lowdown on the best places to visit. I, of course, gave him the number of Battambang's tuk-tuk driver, Ola. Ola just has a better ring to it. Besides, Ola had understood my brief and taken me to the places that gave me a rich rural experience of Cambodia. This, I will always remember and be grateful for.

As for Thean, if I ever visit Battambang again, I promise to hire his services.

4

Culture Queens of Hanoi Show off Their Country

Travel agents the world over are a talkative bunch. I am willing to bet on anything that Lily of the eponymously famed and named Lily Travel Agency in Hanoi is the most talkative of them all. During my three-week stay in Hanoi, Vietnam, I met Lily a bunch of times. And the only time I saw her silent was when she had passed out.

Her tiny frame, flawless skin, impeccable dressing, and sparkling eyes only added to her marketing charm. I soon learned that Lily Travel Agency stood tall and successful on the strong foundation of Lily's loquacious play. What's more, Western tourists loved Lily in a country where fluent English speakers are hard to come by.

I made initial contact with Lily via e-mail on a friend's reference. I expressed my wish to visit a few places around Hanoi, giving her a thorough list of my free days off work. I was on a voluntary English teaching assignment at a vocational training university in Hanoi. Lily assured me that all I needed to do was land up in Hanoi and she would take care of the rest.

I first saw Lily at 6:30 a.m. when I was on my way to Ha Long Bay. A group of sleepy backpackers hung around, waiting at her busy office to board the bus to Ha Long Bay. Red-eyed and groggy, the heavily jetlagged tourists resembled zombies as they stared with empty eyes at Lily as she animatedly marketed a tourist package to an elderly European couple.

I saw Lily again on my return from Ha Long Bay, at 8 p.m. This time, she sat with a bunch of gap-year travellers who were looking for the most efficient and budget-friendly way to optimise their time in Vietnam. Lily was her chattering self. The young travellers left with satisfied smiles and the reassurance that they were not just doing right by their trip to Hanoi but also their every life choice.

Lily makes her clients' travel decisions first and convinces them later. The biggest weapon in her arsenal is her non-stop chatter. I tried to notice her catch a breath. The effort only left me dizzy.

Friends had regaled me with their stories of the Sapa Valley trek as a once-in-a-lifetime experience. So, I approached Lily, of course. From her tiny one-room office in Hanoi's charming Old Quarter, Lily did what she does best—booked me a travel package before I could ask questions. Then she told me to place my implicit trust in her booking skills. I told her that I trusted her completely, and I meant it. Over the next few days, I made a habit of visiting the Old Quarter neighbourhood after work.

Steeped in 1,000 years of history, the Old Quarter is the pulsating commercial heart of Hanoi. Entire alleyways are dedicated to each of the thirty-six business guilds that operate here. Hang means 'street' in Vietnamese. So, Hang Dau means 'the street for oil or petrol businesses'. Similarly, Hang Hanh is where onions are sold, and Hang Gai is where silk shops are lined up. Over the years, these watertight business bifurcations crumbled, making way for hotels and restaurants to accommodate the tourist influx.

I kept returning to the same lanes and bylanes of the Old Quarter for the sensory treat. I would hear incessant honking from motorbikes with riders weaving their way past an impossible web of pedestrian and two-wheeler traffic. A mishmash of people with various purposes walked in crisscross angles. Vendors sold fruits, food, and plasticware on mobile cycle shops. Lost backpackers pored over paper maps at street corners. Especially amusing was the clutch of electrical wires that are balled up on rooftops and atop electric poles on street sides. The wires merge in one big messy tangle tied carelessly to the top of an electric pole.

I smelled warm air mixed with steam rising from the hot food cooked by the street. The concoction of spicy and meaty flavours caused my nostrils to tingle. Familiar fragrances of frankincense and lavender wafted from the lobbies of tiny hotels that clung to the sidewalks.

It was easy to get lost in the warren of lanes here, but it was also easy to find a main street and emerge from the buzzing maze near the Hoan Kiem Lake, the Old Quarter's shining jewel with strong historical roots.

I repeatedly returned to the Old Quarter for its smells and sounds but also for the strange paradox of familiarity in an unfamiliar culture. The streets, the buzz, the sounds, and the pace of life here reminded me so much of the busy shopping street of 8th cross in Malleswaram, Bengaluru. That is where I grew up. For the longest time, my safe space was in that chaos. The streets were always too narrow and there were always too many people. Vendors shouted to lure the shoppers. It was always too noisy. I found home in this chaos.

I would walk by the lake, drink the famous Vietnamese egg coffee, and then drop by at Lily's office, which was in one such narrow alley. Lily told me all about her life, uninhibited about opening up to a stranger. I felt safe to share my stories, too.

One afternoon, Lily looked dull. Her eyes were red and her face seemed tired. But she was still talking to clients and booking their travels. When a client left, I asked about her health.

'Bad headache!' she exclaimed.

I sought permission to massage her temples. She continued speaking as I gently massaged her head. Lily spoke non-stop about the common alternative healing practices and shared a few personal stories as well.

She showed me a video of a healer apparently extracting a soul part from an affected woman. The 'victim' was in dire pain rolling on the floor, screaming incoherently, hair dishevelled. Lily told me that many healers from Indian, Tibetan Buddhist, and other eastern cultures are sought after in Vietnam for alternative healing therapies.

'The celebrities, especially, believe in black magic spells and use these healers for energy protection,' she said.

I only made affirmative sounds to indicate that I was listening to her. As I massaged her for a few more minutes, her words started to slur and then Lily went quiet. There was silence in the office. After about a minute, I felt Lily's head tilting heavily on my right hand. She had passed out. I rested her head on the chair and waited.

After about ten minutes, I woke her up. She opened her eyes, looking fresh and renewed. Those were the only ten minutes I was in the same room as Lily, with no word exchanged between us. The feeling was both strange and fantastic.

Over the weekend, I was excited for my trek to Sapa Valley. I was at Lily's office ironing out the details. I had to reach the Hanoi train station and catch the overnight train to Sapa for a trek up the hills to experience authentic Vietnamese tribal life.

'Where's my ticket?' I asked, to which she said that there would be a woman waiting for me at the train station with my ticket.

'Okay, give me her name and number,' I said, ready to note it down in my book.

'No, she'll find you. Don't worry,' Lily said, in her now-famous reassuring tone. I was concerned.

'How will she find me? Does she have my number?' Lily brushed aside my questions with a wave of her hand and hushed me into calming down.

Her confidence made me look foolish. I didn't want to be that paranoid traveller who plans every last hour of a holiday. So, I acted cool. Maybe Lily had a working system through which her courier was able to match the tickets in hand to the travellers streaming into the busy railway station in Hanoi.

At the bustling train station, I panicked when I saw the crowds and hundreds of passengers rushing in all directions. How is the courier ever going to find me? I went to the waiting room and sat with a thumping heart and racing mind, eagerly bending forward in an attempt to draw attention to myself every time a person walked in, which was every two seconds. I scanned the room with searching eyes. I waited and waited. Now, it was thirty minutes to my train ride. I had to find the platform and my seat on the train.

I called Lily and asked her frantically if the courier was at the station with my ticket. I wasn't prepared to miss this train and spend the weekend in Hanoi. Lily got talking nineteen to the dozen, most of it about telling me to relax. In the midst of her chatter, she told me to step outside the waiting room and look for the steps leading up to the main station building. I did as I was told.

'Now, you will find a woman sitting on the steps. She has your ticket. Happy journey,' she said, before hanging up hurriedly to talk to what sounded like a tense customer in her office.

Indeed, a woman sat on the stairs with a bunch of envelopes in her hand, chewing gum and staring disinterestedly at the crowds. I approached her cautiously not knowing how to ask her if she was a travel agent. She took one look at me and asked: 'Name?' I responded and she started flipping through the envelopes. One had my name on it. I was relieved. I thanked her and ran to find the platform.

The train ride was mostly comfortable. From my upper berth, I watched a mother-daughter duo on the lower berth getting ready for bed. The girl was eight or nine years old. The mother ensured that she changed into pyjamas, brushed her hair, applied face cream, hand cream, and lip balm before she was allowed to lie down and play on the phone.

By the time I woke up, I had reached Sapa. I stepped out into the cool air of the foothills. The majestic hills beckoned, and I felt the anticipation of an invigorating nature trek. A car was supposed to be waiting for me outside the station to take me to the foothills, from where my trek would start. I waited in the midst of a busy arrival area, where vehicles picked up their customers and dashed off into the distance within minutes.

It was 6 a.m. I called Lily. A sleepy Lily answered the phone, but she still sounded like she hadn't stopped talking all night.

'Lily, my transport isn't here,' I told her, unable to mask my irritation.

'Wait, wait. Do you see any van driver there?' she asked. There was one empty van and the driver standing by it looked like he wasn't planning on going anywhere.

I told Lily that, and she asked me to put him on the phone. I gave him my handset. He didn't think it was odd at all. He spoke in Vietnamese. I didn't understand the exchange, but it seemed to be a negotiation. Finally, he returned the phone to me.

'He will take you. Don't worry, I have organised everything,' Lily said, before hanging up.

I enjoyed the hour-long drive across lush green rice fields, cool air brushing my face. The winding mountain roads were no deterrent to the driver being on his phone the entire time. He expertly navigated the curves with one hand on the steering wheel.

At the designated meeting spot, I found my trekking guide, a young woman of about four feet and a few inches. My trekking group was a motley bunch of eight, including three Canadian backpackers, a couple from England, a solo teenage girl from Germany, and two women from Spain. The guide didn't offer introductions.

She took us inside a food market, which was bustling at that early hour. We walked through stalls of meat and more meat. At the end of the indoor complex was a restaurant where she asked us to order anything we wanted. It was part of the package.

We ate in silence and then assembled outside to start the trek. 'Ok, let's go,' was all she said. Nobody else seemed to be curious about the terrain, or how long the trek would be. When I asked her, she shrugged.

'Is it a difficult trek?' I asked.

'No. Very, very easy,' she laughed. I couldn't tell if she was being sarcastic.

All I knew was that we were all heading to Mao's tribal home. Lily promoted this as the definitive rural Vietnam experience. In her office, Lily hung on one wall a huge portrait of a smiling Mao.

We started the climb and soon realised that English, despite the varied accents, was going to be the common thread binding us global trekkers. The trek wasn't allowing for a slow gradient. It started with a steep, almost sixty-degree climb up the thick forest. I was panting in twenty minutes.

'Is the trek this difficult throughout?' I asked the guide between short breaths, to which she only smiled.

In two hours, we reached a scenic valley with lush greenery all around. I saw no trace of human civilisation. There were no electric poles or any walkways or pathways. The hills were tall and majestic, not menacing. I saw almost every shade of green, some that I am sure I was seeing for the first time.

The clear blue sky and rich green swathe together made for a stunning landscape. I saw rice terraces. In August, the season for cultivation, the crops stood tall in their full glory. The beauty was so pristine that I was scared to say anything for fear of contaminating this scenery with my inadequate words. The rest of the group must have felt the same as we walked in silence.

A Canadian man from the group stood at the edge of a cliff and performed a personal ritual. Closing his eyes, he waved his right hand towards the valley as though he was scooping out air from the valley towards his heart. He was taking in positive energy from nature.

The trek continued at a steadier pace, with one hour of steep climb and another hour's flat walking. I was not at my fittest best. Yet, I pushed my body. We were in the middle of nowhere, and I had no choice but to continue walking. By the fourth hour, my body had grown numb to the demands of trekking. I was not even sweating. I just kept going.

I realised somewhere along the way that the guide had not understood my question about how long it would take us to reach the homestay. She knew only a few words in English and couldn't string them together.

I was curious to know how much further we needed to trek and our estimated time of arrival. I asked around but got no answer. Nobody else in the group seemed as curious. They were enjoying the trek, taking in the beauty, stopping to click photos, and admiring the unusual shapes and colours of flowers and leaves.

This made me pause to consider my own attitude to the trek. I was treating this like another assignment, rushing to the finish line. Isn't the purpose of travel to do just the opposite—enjoy the journey and not be keen on arriving? It was at that moment of realisation that I surrendered to the day. This is not a job to finish, it is a journey to experience, I told myself.

When I shifted my mindset, my sensory experience took on dramatically rich tones. The lush green looked fresher when I saw my surroundings through unhurried eyes. I started to notice exotic birds dash across the blue sky. I touched the leaves and flowers along the way. They touched me back with a hello. The air was fresh. I only heard our footsteps and the occasional chirping of birds.

At that moment, my defences were down, my heart open and my senses more alive than they had ever been. My body was responding well to the trek. My knees hurt but were willing to carry me to the destination without fuss.

At the end of the seventh hour of the trek, we reached a waterfall. A bunch of locals were frolicking in the water. This was the most number of people at one place that I had seen since morning. They were enjoying a refreshing afternoon swim at the base of the falls.

I took off my shoes and dipped my feet in the cold water. It sent a healing current of relief through my nerves. I sat in silence and watched the shrieking kids and their indulgent parents. No one was in a hurry to leave this oasis.

The trekking guide told us that the house was only thirty minutes away, and that we should start walking again. So, we collected our things and with dripping-wet clothes, walked the rest of the way.

Mao greeted us from her front door with a big smile and a loud hello in Vietnamese—pronounced *zin chao*. She was four feet nothing, and had fair, glowing skin, chubby cheeks, and a wide smile.

There was an easy air about Mao. She spoke to each one of us as though she knew us from another lifetime. Mao spoke many languages—English, Spanish, German, and a few words of Hindi, too. She was able to switch between languages with ease.

We sat on a patio by the house facing the mighty forest. I sipped on hot tea, which served like a soothing balm for my tired soul.

'Any aches and pains?' Mao enquired after every one of us.

'Full body,' I said, when she asked me, and everyone laughed.

Mao revealed that her plan for the evening was to serve a special Vietnamese drink called 'Happy'. It is a particular favourite of trekkers as the superior pain relief potion, she winked. We understood what she meant and were fine to wait another hour before the sun set.

Mao's was a multi-generational household. The house was a three-hour difficult trek through the forest to the nearest road and any form of transportation. But the house was equipped with modern amenities. It had a television, refrigerator, geyser, kettle, and other needs. I asked Mao how they transported all of these to the house.

'We carry them,' she said, gesturing with her arms stretched over her head to mimic carrying a load.

The house had one bathroom outside the main building. There was no running water. The only thing I needed after that eight-hour strenuous trek was a shower. We waited for two hours. When it got dark, the taps could spew water, finally.

I was the first to rush in for the best shower of my life in that tiny bathroom with broken tiles and a handheld shower, from which water trickled in drops. An elaborate traditional Vietnamese dinner waited for me. Mao made vegetarian spring rolls just for me. We realised how ravenously hungry we were only when the food arrived.

Mao then walked in with a tray full of shot glasses, with the drink called 'Happy'. It was a local rice brew alcohol, pungent and potent. Mao told us the urban legend, perhaps (no, definitely) of her own creation, that whosoever had the Happy drink after a trek in Vietnam would not suffer body aches the following morning. She added that Happy was available only at Mao's homestay.

The trick to making Happy work was in believing. So, I gave it the healing power and drank shot after shot. Then the playing cards came out. With much noise, boisterous revelry, and fun, the party was set to go on deep into the night.

I played a few rounds of cards before slipping out of the house. I went by the outhouse where the dogs rested. Pulling up a chair, I sat beside them looking out into the black night. The stars twinkled in quiet companionship.

An occasional shriek and laughter streamed out of the house. Other than that, I only heard crickets, that quintessential sound of the night. Here I was, in the middle of a thick forest with the stars and trees to accompany my thoughts. I allowed my mind to go wherever it wanted. A substantial amount of Happy was in my belly but I didn't feel its pressure or pull on my mind.

Like I had done earlier in the day during the trek, I surrendered to the moment. I looked back at the events of the day. In the morning, I was completely unaware of where I was going, what experiences would unfold in the day, and how I would respond to them. As the day went by, I checked in about my attitude to the trek and course-corrected with the aim of increasing my joy from this unique exchange with nature.

I managed to complete a difficult trek and as I sat with the night, I was overcome with gratitude. Life's journey is perhaps not that different from going on a long trek. We start with not knowing. Then we build expectations and set goals hoping to achieve money and recognition among other things. But in the end, what makes a journey enjoyable is our own attitude, the attitude of curiosity, an attitude of generosity, the attitude of gratitude and the attitude of joy for the sake of joy.

The stillness of the night enveloped me, wrapping me in a tight hug. At that moment, I felt no regret or guilt, no judgment or criticism. I felt gratitude and acceptance of my choices and my experiences as unique, special and, stoically, essential.

The leaves rustled in agreement. It took the trek and my need to steal this quiet moment to feel a connection with the ground beneath me and the stars above, at this special place. That is all it takes to make a mindset shift, sometimes.

I sat in silence for a long time, till the card games got louder and louder. Time to celebrate my life now, I told myself, and went inside to join the noise. The revelry broke up around 2 a.m. when the trekkers started slipping away into their bedrooms for well-deserved rest.

The next day, fresh as the morning sun, we started the trek back after a sumptuous breakfast of pancakes. Mao led us back to the road this time.

'Should we take the longer or shorter route?' she asked.

'Longer,' said the group in unison. I was the only one that said 'shorter'. We laughed and took the longer route.

The landscapes were bright in the morning freshness. Where there was no path, we walked on slush. We crossed waterfalls. We cut through rice fields. And we reached the town from where the bus would take us to the train station.

Mao tied a friendship band on my wrist as a reminder of her friendship, and of this trek. For me, this will always be the trek that made me surrender. With that sentiment, I took the train back to Hanoi.

When I met Lily, I hugged her tight for recommending Sapa Valley. I promised to recommend her travel services to all my friends. After all, a little adventure never hurt anyone.

I SURRENDER

What we cannot let go of while at home, we sometimes surrender in a new place among strangers and in the midst of unfamiliar emotions. Travel has been about learning to let go both gently or with force, as the situation demanded. The more I held on, the more I realised I was turning against my best interest. With surrender came peace. In this section, I write about surrendering my body image, difficult emotions, expectations, habits, the need for company, and—the most difficult of them all—surrendering to the moment.

5

A Solo Trek in Zurich Tests Emotional Mettle

Clichés come alive in Switzerland. I had chocolate, fondue, watches, and snow-capped mountains on my mind when I arrived in Zurich, the busy financial district. In a few hours ambling about town, I saw streetside cafes, narrow winding cobblestone alleyways, boutiques, people cycling everywhere, plazas with sculptures, watch towers, motorboats rushing down the river, and tall men in black suits carrying slim briefcases, half-sprinting with purpose into glass-facade offices.

I had heard enough about Zurich's avant-garde, arty vibe and hipster charm and was curious, but my heart was set on a trek in the countryside.

In an emerging tourist trend, Swiss farmers offered cow trekking trails for adventurous tourists to ride dairy cows. Intriguing as it was, I gave it a miss and decided, instead, to take the cable car, a first, and go on a solo trek.

I ditched the urban edge in favour of Switzerland's rural beauty. I hopped on at the Adliswil Luftseilbahn Station and rode the cable car for ten minutes to Felsenegg. This car became operational in 1954 and took me to a height of over 800 metres above sea level and about 450 metres above the city.

The ride was everything I had imagined it to be—a steep incline in a pod suspended mid-air, gently bobbing from side to side. I was looking down at my feet for the first few minutes to get used to the movement, the steady hum and the pace.

With a deep breath, I lifted my head up and looked through the scratched and fogged-up glass windows and immediately let out a sigh at the breathtaking landscapes of the city far below. The buildings were like miniature toys. I could see trees, buildings, tiny people, and a flowing river. They all looked like miniature toys. It was a scenery straight out of a painting.

I reached the end of my ride and followed the signs to Planetenweg, the starting point of the hike to Uetliberg. It would be a two-hour hike. I was well prepared with a water bottle, chocolates, snacks, and a hand towel. I had a map in my backpack but didn't think I would need it considering that this was a marked trail. I planned to walk at a moderate speed.

I had everything I needed. There was nothing to do but to start walking. This was the first solo trek of my life. I was anxious. Out of anxiousness, I started an internal dialogue.

Many things could go wrong in the wilderness but here I was. The only way to conquer fear is to face it. Unless you walk the path, you will never know. And I really wanted to know how far I could take the fear with me. I was hoping to abandon it along the trail somewhere. Another voice asked why I was doing this at all. It was to face my fears. It was to cross imaginary borders. It was to push my limits.

I walked on, carrying the anxiousness within me along with a deep sense of curiosity for what was on the other side of this hike. I was testing the waters of solo trekking in these early years and was undecided about my feelings towards it. Will I enjoy it? What will I do by myself? Will I be safe? Will I be bored? Am I interesting enough to be with me for this long?

The pathway was mostly flat, with a few inclines and declines, but never too steep. The forest pathway opened up to a landscape where Zurich stretched out below with the Limmat river slicing through the crop of concrete.

Benches made from tree logs sat at the forest edge offering uninterrupted views of the horizon at the distance. The cityscape was a part of this scenery. If I squinted, I could catch the movement of buses and people. I strained to hear something, anything. But I only heard the occasional swish of the leaves and the gentle whoosh of the wind.

The quiet was uncomfortable, making me wish for company. I wanted to be in the midst of the city buzz, people, and of familiar sounds. Did I make a mistake with this trek? Was I too adventurous for my own good? I seriously wondered.

But there was no turning back now. I walked on, humming along to mask the rising discomfort. Was it the discomfort with my own company? Or the silence around me? The path spread up to flatlands with lush green grass, a single thatched-roof house in the midst of the grass bed, and snow-capped mountains in the backdrop, all making for a picture-postcard landscape.

It was July, a beautiful time to be in Switzerland, where the sun shone bright and people looked cheerful. Though I walked for a long time under the sun, I didn't feel the heat or fatigue that typically accompanies long hours spent in sunlight in tropical climes.

I continued walking in silence for about forty-five minutes, not a soul in sight. My feet were happy, not tired at all with the trek. Till now, I had not seen a single person or animal. I had spotted a few birds along the way. I will take a long shot and say I saw a magpie but I couldn't be sure.

At one point, I slowed down at a steep incline and stopped to take a sip of water. I hadn't still seen anyone, yet I did not feel unsafe. All I knew was that I had to keep going and that it was okay to be by myself.

My feet were steady on the path, but my mind started to wander, sometimes to the past and within a fraction of a second to the future. My mind opened the memory box of my most embarrassing moments. Remember the time you bought and wore a t-shirt with the Playboy rabbit logo on it, my mind asked? I grunted aloud: 'I didn't know what it was,' and then looked around. There was nobody to hear me. I wore the t-shirt to a casual party and recalled the giggles, the raised eyebrows, and the curious looks directed at me. The worst was the come-hither looks from men. I felt my cheeks get warmer now as they had at the party when someone finally told me what I had done.

Remember the time you let one rip in a yoga class? Remember the time when you went to the Hooters restaurant in the US and didn't think much of the waitresses' dress of orange shorts and ribbed tank tops with cleavage bursting forth? Remember wondering why all the groups of men stared at you from their tables? 'The place is known for its sex appeal and the waitresses are called Hooters Girls,' my colleague explained. I nodded as though it was a great cultural insight when deep down I felt mortified by my ignorance.

Remember the time you arrived at the wrong wedding venue? Remember when you confidently used the wrong word with the opposite meaning of your intended message on stage during a speech? Remember . . . I pressed my palms over my ears to shut out the noise within.

This was harder than I thought. Silence is not for everyone. Solitude is not joyful for everyone, I thought. I didn't think I would ever begin to enjoy my own company. I started to hum old Hindi songs to drown out the words forming in my mind.

After a few minutes, at a distance, I spotted a cluster of houses with cows scattered and grazing in the fields. To see living beings, even if they were cows, was comforting to my interaction-starved spirit—even if it had only been an hour.

Here was another Switzerland cliché coming alive before my eyes. The cows had the traditional Swiss bells around their necks. They looked clean and content. I stopped to see if they would turn to look at me or moo in acknowledgment, but they did not. They were busy grazing, and I felt foolish marvelling at cows, considering I come from a country where cows are everywhere.

I walked on and saw every shade of green along the rolling hills, punctuated by trees and shrubs along the way. And then, I saw him. A man wearing a checked shirt, jeans and hat came into view at a distance. He walked towards me.

I was preparing to give him my best smile and hoped for a chat. If not a chat, then it would be a smile or a nod, I hoped. He walked closer. I looked at him and away and again towards him with the intention of seeming cool. We got within a few feet of each other. I looked at him and smiled but he didn't even look up, continuing to walk with purpose towards his destination.

Disappointed, I continued walking. I was going to be my own company on this trek. That became clear. I could see in this short trek the metaphor for how we go through life craving company, expecting someone to come and fill our loneliness. Being alone reminds us that the only person we will always be with, no matter what the changing circumstances, is ourselves.

At the end of nearly two hours of silence and no human beings in sight, I craved to see faces and hear voices, even if in a foreign language.

This first solo trek, although short and not physically demanding, had given me a taste of how much my inner strength needed work if I wanted to travel more, that, too, solo. It revealed just how uncomfortable I was by myself. I realised that this had to change. I already knew that I didn't enjoy noisy discotheques or man-made centres of entertainment where external sounds drowned out the inner silence. But what I didn't know was that I did not respond well to quiet and calming places in nature either. The silence brought out my demons even more strongly.

This short trek taught me that I needed to address these demons. There was much that I had to surrender for more exciting paths to open up before me. I had to surrender fear, first and foremost. I had to surrender the desire for comfort. I had to make friends with the unfamiliar. I had to surrender expectations and open up to life's miraculous synchronicities. I had to surrender control. I had to surrender my fixed mindset. In surrendering so much, I would lay the foundation for a life in which I would learn to flow like water. This was not easy. Moreover, how badly did I want this?

I was at a mental crossroads at this point—one path would take me further along self-discovery by working with and through the uncomfortable inner silence; the other path would make me retreat to a place of physical comfort, where I decide that I am probably not cut out for solo travel because it shows me a clean mirror to myself, and I don't yet want to see a reflection of the real me.

I chose the first, more difficult path.

Symbolically, towards the end of this chat with myself, I reached the bottom of the steep stairs leading to the

Uetliberg peak. I took one step at a time in a steady and strong manner. I was about to reach the end of the path, and there I saw a top view of Zurich, where nature and city blended into one glorious landscape. I took in the scenery but I could not stand there for too long. It was not the time to pause. It was the time to keep moving.

I caught the bus back to the city, and into the comforting company of strangers and the sounds of the city. Switzerland was a dream destination fulfilled, stirring a deep desire to better understand myself and that lacunae in my spirit. In that, I will hardly remember Switzerland as a cold place. I always have a warm corner of my heart reserved for Switzerland.

6

Crossing a Threshold in Tayshet with a Naked Body, Bare Soul, and Birch Leaves

I stood stark naked in front of the full-length mirror observing my curves. I needed to lose my stress paunch. Also, my waist could do with a few inches of toning. My thighs were feeling ignored due to erratic exercise and schedule. A few days of regular yoga and a mindful diet should bring my body to a desirably toned and healthy look.

I could stare at my nakedness for hours without feeling bored or encountering emotions of shame or dislike about my physique. I liked my body and I was comfortable with it. I didn't need any of the now-trending body confidence classes that taught the urban-educated, comparison-fuelled anxious minds to accept their body for what it was. Then what was I worried about? Was it the discomfort about being naked in front of a stranger? Probably, I told myself.

But I am naked in front of the masseuse, the hair removal specialist, and the doctor—people with whom I have no plans to be intimate with. Here's a stranger in a foreign country whom I will probably never meet again. And he, like these professionals, is only doing his job.

And so my mind reasoned with the creeping discomfort, to settle it for good. I was now going to experience the world-famous Russian steam bath—not in a commercial urban tourist trap but in a Siberian *banya* (sauna) in the tiny Russian village-town of Tayshet—with only the male house owner for company.

I had met Igor Shalygin on a Facebook group that brought together aspiring Trans-Siberian railway travellers and experts who could guide those travellers. Igor spoke of the beauty that is Tayshet, which also carried an important slice of Russian history in the Gulag system of forced labour camps in the 1930s. I made a quick stopover at Tayshet on the BAM (Baikal-Amur Mainline) train, before continuing along the Trans-Siberian route.

Tayshet was a seven-hour whistle-stop tour that included a short hike up a hill to see the top view of the village, a church visit, a drive along a historic Russian highway, and paying tribute at the cemetery where the Gulag victims were laid to rest. I drank local Russian vodka, shopped at a grocery store for supplies to carry on the train, and ate a wholesome homemade meal.

This small town packed quite a punch. But I will always remember Tayshet as the town where I experienced the unforgettable authentic Russian steam bath. It was also the town where I conquered a fear—the fear of being judged for my body.

I was unsure how my body would react to the intense heat from the steam, and I didn't want to be uncomfortable before a long train journey. The ideal state would have been to rest on a comfortable bed with some vodka in my belly rather than waggle all night on a train berth.

I expressed my uncertainty to Igor. He would have none of it. 'I promise you that you will not get this experience in the city. They have corrupted the authentic experience with modern gadgets and by allowing people to wrap towels around them. I mean, who wears a towel to a banya?' he scoffed.

'Trust me, you will never get to do this again,' he was so sure of it. He also put down the rules very clearly. We were going to be completely naked in the steam bath. That was the only way to experience and benefit from the bath.

My sense of adventure was far greater than all my apprehensions, including the ones about my naked body, put together. I was ready for the experience. I wrapped myself in a towel and waited for Igor.

'Is anyone else going to join us?' I asked him.

'No, it's just us,' he said.

Per Igor's instructions, I carried towels, shampoo, soap, and a fresh set of clothes. The banya was in a detached outhouse across the lawns from the main house. It was a wooden standalone structure with an outer and inner room.

The moment I entered the outer room, I was wrapped in a warm hug by the toasty air. I saw a wooden bench and pegs on the wall to hang clothes. One side of the fairly large room was used as a storage area for unused household things. Igor had already set up the banya and excitedly asked me if I was ready to go in. I clapped in excitement.

Igor took off his bathrobe and hung it on the clothes peg. I unwrapped my towel and hung it on another peg.

'Let's go,' he said.

It was as simple as that. I was amused by the ease of the moment—all that build-up of emotions and thoughts were for this exact moment, which went by without pause or fuss. There wasn't even any background music to accompany the act of standing naked in front of a stranger. I was a tad disappointed about that.

'We are now standing in the *predbannik* or the outer relaxation room. We come here to get respite from the heat in the *parilka* or the steam room,' Igor said pointing to the door beyond which stood the heart of the famed Russian banya. He said that the predbannik is not temperature-controlled. The traditional banya has a third room called the *moyka*, which is the washroom.

The banya has great cultural and spiritual significance in Slavic regions. Practitioners alternate between jumping in the snow or chilled water and then getting the extreme steam treatment thereby releasing adrenaline and stress hormones.

Regular banya treatment readies the body for greater immunity while releasing toxins. The Russians also believe that the banya helps the body release stuck emotions and cleanse the energies to, truly, make the body come out of the steam room spanking clean.

As he spoke, I noticed that he wasn't at all focused on my nakedness. Nor did he care that he was, too. I looked straight at his face with a serious expression that befits a keen student of banya culture.

I stepped into the parilka with a cautious sense of purpose. I was instantly assaulted by a tidal wave of heat. It surprised me, making it difficult to breathe in the dense air. My breathing went shallow and sweat trickled out of every pore of my body in protest.

When I somewhat adjusted to the laboured breathing, I looked around. It was a much smaller room compared to the predbannik. The floor was covered in wooden slats. In the far corner of the room stood two long wooden benches made of slats. They were layered, like the seating at an arena. Igor asked me to take a seat and explained the workings of the banya.

'See this fire here?' he pointed to a stove. The fire was contained in an iron bucket on which were mounted large stones. Igor took a bucket of water and splashed it on the stones. Steam hissed from the stones covering the entire room in thick fog. The room became even warmer and my sweat mingled with the steam. We waited in silence for the steam to settle.

'This steam is good for the body. It improves blood circulation and is good for controlling blood pressure and workings of the kidney,' explained Igor, as I bore the discomfort of the heat.

We sat in silence for five minutes, soaking up the heat. Sweat was pouring like streams from every part of my body. It was a strangely warm and fuzzy feeling, in which I felt alive.

We then stepped out to the predbannik to the contrasting cool air. My body thanked me for the respite. My skin came alive with the hot-cold contrast. It was rejuvenating to have the skin pores open and respond to the changing temperature.

Now Igor spoke some more. 'When the heat gets too uncomfortable, you step out for some relief. Then you go back in. You shouldn't stay in either room for over ten minutes,' he said. We did this for two more rounds, with more steam rising from the hot stones.

The provenance of the banya is not attributed to one culture or geography alone. It appears in different parts of the world as a body-cleansing system that makes pain and sadness go away. In Russia, people take a hot steam bath and immediately jump into a cold lake or river or snow to refresh the body.

In Russian history, banyas attained political significance as businessmen and politicians used the informal setting to forge alliances and close deals. The banya had none of the stuffiness of an office environment, and so was considered a relaxed place to change minds and sign deals.

Igor brought out the birch leaves, the '*Vennik*' in local parlance, a bath broom made of birch, oak or fir leaves. These dried leaves were dunked in a bucket of hot water. He asked me to lie down on the top wooden bench and slapped my body with the Vennik. It tickled me to no end, and I didn't control my laughter, but Igor didn't find it funny.

'This is good for cleaning the pores and any bad energy you may have. Steam is fantastic for curing any illness. It is tradition to take an ice-cold shower between steam baths. It prepares the body for extremes of the Siberian climate,' he said.

We did these rounds between the predbannik and parilka a few more times. And I got slapped with the birch leaves again. 'Are all banyas like this? Or are there modern versions?' I asked Igor. He spoke passionately against the commercialisation of steam baths in the cities. Nor did he agree with gender-specific banyas.

'Why do we need separate banyas for men and women? And what is the point of covering yourself? How will you get the benefit of the banya?' he said.

Igor also didn't agree with the modern banyas that generated steam through electricity. 'That defeats the entire purpose!' he exclaimed. He again told me that this was the way a traditional banya is done. He reiterated that he was happy to share this unique experience with me.

We went into the parilka for one last round, after which he left to the house to shower and change, leaving me alone with the thoughts of the banya. I felt refreshed unlike any other time of my life. My body felt as though it had been turned inside out and scraped of all the grime and stuck emotions. I felt lightheaded. I had been reset.

As I dressed, I laughed over my internal dialogue over my nakedness. It was important because I made it important.

Igor didn't care about being bare-bodied, also perhaps because he was so accustomed to this practice.

First times are always special because they always happen only once. In my first experience of the banya, I shed not only my clothes but also the social conditioning over the 'correctness' of protecting my modesty. Nakedness is in the mind more than it is anywhere else. Similarly, the lack of decency is also in the mind more than it is anywhere else.

In shutting down the mental chatter to embrace my body in all its curves and imperfections, I had surrendered to my higher self in the moment. This surrender was an act of defiance, albeit a quiet one in the privacy of my own company, almost. Most big decisions happen this way. It is these seemingly small decisions, often made in silence, that are more impactful and capable of sustaining than any loud, chest-thumping declaration.

In that one afternoon, I had surrendered my body confidence issues—my inhibitions about physical nakedness as well as my deeper spirit—for a thorough cleansing. I trusted that the experience in a wooden shack would do the job. The belief set the tone for the highest surrender, and it mattered more than anything.

7

Berlin is a City in Bardo

Berlin is a city with a troubled past. During my short visit to Germany, I was keen to peep into this darkness just a tad. I wanted to relive a bit of her history to better understand Germany through the future she chose for herself. I signed up for one of the many popular city-walking tours one afternoon. But before that, I visited the Holocaust Memorial, the Memorial to the Murdered Jews of Europe.

The memorial had opened in May 2005, only a few months before my visit to Berlin, which I found surprising. What could have taken so long to create this place? When I reached the memorial, I was confused by what I saw.

Grey cement slabs were spread out on a large tract of open area. It looked, at first, like a cemetery. I walked closer, thinking that perhaps each slab had a name on it. But I saw nothing. These were blocks of rectangular cement, placed erratically in rows and columns. Each cement block was a unique size, different from the others in height, width, and placement. There seemed to be no apparent order or organisation to the placement of these blocks. I was intrigued and walked closer to understand what this artwork was conveying.

I walked through the memorial, with the blocks on either side. As I walked further in, the ground sloped downward and the slabs grew taller around me. *Okay, so this is a sensory experience*, I thought, and walked around erratically between blocks—up and down, left, and right.

At one point, I saw these grey chunks everywhere, as far as the eye could see. There seemed to be nothing beyond. It was terrifying, even if for a little while, and it made me uncomfortable. I knew that it wasn't easy to lose my way here. This was not a maze, and there were people around. Still, I felt a strange sense of foreboding.

I continued walking down the slope. The blocks grew taller and taller, and the ground gradually sloped downward. Now the blocks were as tall as me, and the next moment, they were taller. Their placement also required me to walk in a zigzag manner.

With imposing grey blocks all around, I could not take it anymore. I am not claustrophobic, but I felt as though these cement chunks were closing in on me. I couldn't breathe, and I needed to get out into free space, the light, open air, and safety. I started walking back up the slope, my breathing still laboured. It took some effort to zigzag my way through the erratic and haphazardly placed blocks.

I felt like I was underwater, out of air, and out of options. I was nauseated and unsettled in a deep way, which I did not expect at all. I expected to feel sorrow and reflection, mulling the path that world history had taken, all from a safe emotional distance. I was not prepared to plunge into the depths of helplessness and vulnerability.

As I walked up to a place where the blocks came up to my waist or below, I sighed deeply in relief. I was shaken by this unforeseen experience of terror; it was not pretty. Taking a moment to rest my racing heart and settle the nausea rising from my belly, I looked up at the deep-blue, almost cloudless sky, wading in its inviting vastness.

The memorial was built on a tract of land on which once stood the Berlin Wall. I imagined the wall crumbling and rearranging into the haphazardly placed 2,711 rectangular stones that remember the wronged. It was a merging of the intellectual and the emotional for architect Peter Eisenman who conceived this design.

I sat with a range of emotions, many of them unfamiliar to me. The emotions that I had earlier understood only from an intellectual angle now became a real-life experience at this site. For example, I had experienced helplessness before. Here, I experienced helplessness at a deep level, giving me a taste of what I would feel in my body and mind when there were no more options left. Or worse, what it felt like, perhaps, to not be empowered enough to exercise any option.

I felt the familiar emotions to a heightened extent, which made them, contrarily, unfamiliar. Everything was exaggerated. In this fragile moment, I intuitively drifted towards surrender. Standing up to these difficult emotions of powerlessness, fear and blocked paths was going to be both useless and impossible. I had no option but to gather all the rising difficult feelings, bundle them up in a ball, and release them to the blue sky.

Connecting with the Collective

In walking between the stone slabs, I had unknowingly signed up to feel deep empathy for the Holocaust victims. To set foot on this land was one thing, and to live the experience was another. This was the sensory experience that dismissed the details in favour of heightening the senses.

The names were less important. Who was the perpetrator and who was the victim became insignificant. It was futile to look at numbers of how many died. All that mattered was the experience of this time from the past.

Right there, I experienced the deepest empathy for the unknown and unseen. I was dipping into the depths of a vast pool of powerlessness to have a slice of that ordeal. For those of us who think 'I will never know what the victims went through', this exhibit is an attempt to make you feel only a sliver of the dominant collective emotion of the oppressed and the victimised.

What I had only read about in history books came alive in an experiential form where an intellectual understanding was parked aside in favour of the emotional trial. In this, I believe that empathy is the hallmark of travel and, for that matter, all interaction. How much do we truly *feel* another being?

I had set foot in Germany; I had seen the land. But right there, I experienced its history in the most intimate way. I walked away from that memorial with my emotions stirred in a difficult concoction. Difficult, because what I felt was not entirely my own. What I felt there came from a collective past that was not rationally aligned to my current life experience. At that moment, I was living someone else's emotions without knowing why or how. I didn't try to unpack my feelings then. I just needed to get out of there.

Before leaving, I knew that I had to surrender those emotions that had risen. Carrying them in my heart and head would be too heavy for me. Taking a deep breath, I was attempting to release the unknown out into space. This was a type of surrender where the outcome was unclear. These emotions were not mine, and I was letting them go with the hope to heal—myself as well as a tiny part of history that had come alive in me.

I had to release the grip and trust that something better would take over and, like a cloud of smoke let out into the open, allow an ending and, from there, a new beginning to emerge. I had to find my oasis of peace within myself. Part of that process was to trust without seeing or knowing and simply believing.

Surrender has the power to release us from the burden of stress and worry. I was releasing any uncomfortable emotions, imagining them as grey smoke rising in a swirling dance before turning completely invisible in seconds. Poof! They were gone. And I was searching for calm within.

At that moment, I felt as though I was connecting to something greater than myself. I had emotionally moved ahead from this experience, and I had to physically move, too.

I visited the exhibits at the lower level of the memorial, where the story of the Holocaust unfolded in images and text. I half-heartedly walked past all the exhibits more as a matter of being there and less out of genuine curiosity. I left to sit out under the sun on the green grass opposite the Brandenburg Gate. Never before had the touch of cool grass under the warm sunshine felt so comforting. Mother Earth held me in her tight embrace. Grateful for the ability to sense the heartbeat of the earth, I stayed for a few more moments like an infant in the womb.

In Bardo

It was time for some social interaction and to see the other sides of Berlin. The city was full of visible and not-so-apparently-visible symbols of borders, crossings, and crossing over.

Through its deeply disturbing history, I saw Berlin as a transit lounge to both hell and heaven. In it, I saw the soul of a city with dramatic endings and the possibility of many beginnings.

Berlin was in bardo, but she was not stuck. She was moving and making room for transformation. The rest of what I saw in Berlin proved this.

I signed up for a walking tour and met a bunch of tourists to discover the city some more. Mark, an enthusiastic young man with a strong English accent, not much older than thirty, led the motley group. A chatty couple from England, in their sixties, was curious about my life in India. They asked me many questions. Are you taught English in school, or did you have to take special lessons? You are here alone? And your parents are okay with that? Do you get to choose what to study? Are there shopping malls in your country?

I patiently answered as we walked from the Pariser Platz, a square by the Brandenburg Gate, down the Unter den Linden Boulevard. We made stops at the Berlin State Library, the Reichstag building and the Neue Wache, the Central Memorial of the Federal Republic of Germany for the Victims of War and Dictatorship, all located in the central Mitte district.

Whether it was the building in Bebelplatz where the Nazis banned books on fire in 1933, or the famous Checkpoint Charlie, that historic crossing of the border between East and West Berlin, power, control, and the struggle for freedom were all embedded in every layer of German history.

Then there was the Berlin Wall, first with the building and then the undoing. The main section of the graffiti-heavy wall is protected behind glass. When the official demolition of the wall started in 1990, over 40,000 of its sections were recycled for use in construction projects across Germany. Fragments of the historic wall have taken on new life in other parts of the world. A few hundred sections were auctioned off, with one section in Rome's Vatican Gardens, and another in a men's urinal at Main Street Station Casino, Las Vegas. Even as one slice of history ended in Berlin, it remains alive and frozen, merging with other histories.

Berlin was the city where the process of building and breaking down was taking place almost simultaneously. It is the bardo after death and before birth.

I experienced an invisible element of Berlin's history on its streets at a car park.

Mark, the guide, led the group to a car park and dramatically asked, 'Anyone knows why we are here?'

We all looked around and shrugged. We had seen the historic buildings and the checkpoints as a matter of fact. Mark was pausing here and making a point about this place. Cars drove in and out. Nobody noticed anything unusual.

'During the Nazi regime, there used to be an underground bunker below this very parking space. It was in that bunker that Hitler shot himself,' said Mark in a slow, deliberate, and dramatic manner, looking into our eyes and pausing a few seconds for effect. There was silence as we each tried to dramatise the scene in our minds.

The walking tour ended in four hours. I walked slowly, taking in the vibe of the streets. Its energy left me pensive and longing for calming silence. The events of the day, the stirring of emotions, even just that quick dip into Germany's history, left me thoughtful. I wanted to return home. I appreciated more than ever that I had a home I could return to.

8

Two-Minute Friends Create Memories of a Lifetime On the Trans-Siberian

The train ride from Ulan-Ude to Slyudyanka was loud, and it sounded like a party was afoot in the wagon. Two women and a man, all in their seventies, joked non-stop like they were long-lost friends. They had only just met in the train but that didn't prevent them from engaging in intense conversation between frequent squeals of laughter. The man chugged shot after vodka shot in his transparent coffee mug which had yellow flowers printed on it. After every glug, he laughed louder and louder.

I sat watching in amusement because the typical stereotype of Russian brusqueness was broken here with their guard down and inhibitions cracked open by the heady mix of alcohol and the train's rhythmic swaying.

This was the Platzkartny, the open-plan carriage in which six passengers share a cubicle—four at the centre and two single side berths. Platzkartny wagons are typically friendlier, open, and attract people who engage in the joys of travelling together to the same destination. Comparatively, the second-class coupé with four passengers shut in a room can be uptight and claustrophobic if stuck with snotty passengers, or heavy snorers, depending on your luck.

I was glad to be in jovial company although I didn't understand a word they said. I felt included in this group of strangers. When they cracked jokes and laughed, they each gave me subtle sideways glances to have me join the laughter. In those split seconds that each of them looked at me, they were laughing with me and wanted me to join. Laughing was more important than the laughter being meaningful.

The result was that I didn't bury my nose in a book, stare out the window, or take a nap as I typically do on train rides. I was with them in spirit and mood throughout the trip, smiling when they laughed, rejoicing in the merriment. Never so clearly have I understood inclusion, be it in physical space, language, class, ethnicity, or cultural barriers. Intent is revealed in everything that we do, most of all in behaviour and actions. Here, my co-travellers intended to include me in their impromptu party, and I felt included.

When I got off at Slyudyanka, this group of jolly elderly train companions gave me the loudest send-off waving goodbyes and blowing kisses in my direction. I stood on the platform continuing to wave back at them as the train pulled out of the station.

That was it, a brief encounter that broke the limiting stereotype that I held about the Russian people. This was a stereotype I had reiterated, sometimes to comic effect and oftentimes to oversimplify my view of the Russians. I thought I had understood them over a month of my travels across their country. Yet, here was a bunch of smiling strangers telling me that I have not figured them out, and that I probably never will. Painting them all with the same brushstroke is a rookie mistake I was making, they were showing.

Even the briefest of meetings can leave lasting impressions on the mind and heart. A few hours on a local train with the locals would now give me pause every time I attempted to describe the Russians in sweeping generalisations.

I was greeted by a light snow shower and heavy wind chills when I walked out of the station into the blue twilight hour. A small town with a population of under 20,000, Slyudyanka was my brief stopover before catching another train the next morning.

The town was deserted and not a vehicle drove by its only main street. I walked in the general direction of the guesthouse where I had a reservation for the night. The buildings didn't have numbers, nor were street names apparent even if they were listed somewhere.

I did not have phone data connection, and even if I did, I didn't speak the language. What a pickle I was in, I thought to myself. I wore my gloves, cap, and pulled my scarf tighter around my neck against the biting cold.

After about five minutes, a tall man with Middle Eastern features walked in my direction wrapped in a black leather jacket and boots, gloves, and a woollen cap. He didn't even look up toward me. So, I had to call out to him and point to the address on a slip of paper. He read the address and looked in both directions of the empty road, clueless. Pulling out a phone from his back pocket, he made a couple of phone calls.

Standing in the biting cold, I felt most vulnerable with no option but to surrender to a complete stranger in a strange land. I was a solo traveller, new to this town, and not a soul had seen me here. There was potential for a lot to go wrong in this situation. But I had no choice other than to allow this situation to play out.

'Where are you from?' I typed on the translator on my phone to start an awkward conversation with using technology.

'Kyrgyzstan,' he said, not smiling or attempting to ask me any questions. I asked him more questions and found that he had moved to Russia six years ago and had made Slyudyanka home.

We waited for a few minutes in silence after which his phone rang. Still talking on the phone, he walked briskly in the opposite direction from where he came. I was meant to follow him, so I half-ran to catch up.

We saw a slender, sharply dressed woman walking towards us. He left me in the care of this woman, who showed me a copy of my reservation on her phone. I have never sighed so loudly in relief. She was the guesthouse owner. I wasn't being kidnapped or taken for a ride. The man didn't even wait to say goodbye, turning and walking away so quickly that I couldn't tell if my thank yous in both English and Russian reached his ears.

In that moment, I felt like running after him and saying thank you, but the guesthouse lady had already turned and was briskly walking in the opposite direction. The freezing cold makes people want to get indoors as quickly as possible. They walk faster and don't linger outdoors without reason.

I wish I could have thanked him. He didn't need it but I did. I needed to tell him that the gesture of helping me find my destination may have been a small one for him. For me, he had just laid another brick in the wall of confidence that not all is lost in the world. He had just shown me that kind people exist, and that there are still people out there sprinkled in parts of the world who would do a favour without asking for anything in return, not even a thank you.

A few weeks later, I was stuck in a similar situation in Novosibirsk, but it was daytime in a crowded train station with thousands of people crisscrossing my path. I was negotiating the rate for a short taxi ride with a driver using only hand gestures. The driver was testing my patience by not agreeing to a reasonable price and yet not moving on to another customer either.

Fed up with the no-words negotiation, I said out loud more to myself: '80 Rubles. Not more.'

A young man in his late teens who was watching from a corner smiled and walked towards us. He dismissed the taxi driver and spoke to me in fluent English. 'Where do you need to go?' he asked.

I shared the address, and he said, 'I'll show you.'

He said that he was walking in the opposite direction, but he is willing to walk with me to show me the place. 'You don't need a taxi. It's an easy ten-minute walk.'

'Don't you have somewhere else to be?' I asked.

'I have to meet my mother for lunch. But it's okay to go ten minutes later. By walking with you, I can practise my English,' he said.

Vadim, a nineteen-year-old college student, was interested to study English and perhaps someday teach the language.

'Not many people here speak English,' I commented, to which he laughed and said, 'Now you know why I want to talk with you.'

He spoke about his sister's fascination with India. 'She watches Bollywood dances on YouTube all the time and tries to learn the steps.'

We talked about Novosibirsk in relation to bigger Russian cities like Moscow and smaller places in Siberia and Crimea regions.

'The big brands are now everywhere but this city is still like a small town despite all these fancy stores you see here,' he said pointing to a long line of lifestyle shops.

It turned out that my guesthouse was tucked away inside a building that didn't have a signboard. It was another obstacle before I could reach my room, which Vadim sorted by making a call and finding the exact entrance for me. Flashing a bright smile, Vadim waved me good luck before turning and walking cheerfully away.

This time, I had been in a position to offer a good Samaritan something—my company—in exchange for his help. Although it felt comforting to meet a kind stranger halfway, I became acutely aware that I was misunderstanding this exchange as a transactional one.

How could I ever quantify the joy of listening to the story of a young Russian man while walking down Novosibirsk's main avenue? And, for that matter, how could he quantify the chance meeting with an Indian woman, a rather rare occurrence for someone who hasn't ever left his city? Vadim doesn't know if time could make him cross the seas in future. I was that stranger who came into town bringing with me a bagful of stories and cultural notes.

Most experiences in life cannot be measured. In a rather poor attempt at commerce, we try to calculate everything from the steps we take each day to the calories we eat. The joy derived from a walk in the woods or a deep conversation with an empathetic friend are treasures that we cannot put a price on.

Travel, more than any other form of spirituality, teaches us this. We move and pass through, briefly or for a bit longer, people's lives when there is a give and take. The exchange can never be quantified. This is the reason some encounters are special. They leave us more knowledgeable while some show us that all we have is this present moment.

Back on the train, I met Russians who lived joyfully in the moment. On one ride, a man in his twenties climbed on to the top berth and fell asleep even before the train left the station. He woke up two hours later, fresh from a satisfying nap, and sat next to me starting a conversation that bordered on the flirtatious. We didn't speak the same language but that didn't prevent either of us from continuing the conversation.

Viktor was the son of a farmer in Severobaikalsk who was studying in Irkutsk and was taking the train up there to meet his family at the dacha. Dacha is a summer home, where most Russian upper- and middle-class families still spend summers. It is a country house with a garden plot where families spend summertime growing vegetables and crops that would last them a long time into the winter.

'It is a family tradition now. We Russians use the time to spend with family,' he explained through the translator.

When he got to know that I get off the train in only a few hours, he gave me advice on things to see and do in the western Russian cities. Our chat done, he promptly climbed to his berth to continue his nap.

On another train ride, I met an English teacher in her fifties, who was visiting her son in the city for the summer. It was a relief that I didn't have to use the phone translator to talk to this pleasant-looking woman with a gentle smile. She taught English to third-grade students and had a patient and deliberate manner. She, like every other Russian woman that I saw on the train, was particular about make-up. Irrespective of age or social class, I saw women spending at least fifteen minutes applying make-up either as soon as they woke up or as soon as they got on the train. It was an integral part of their routine, like brushing teeth or taking a shower.

On the same ride, I met a plumber, who was a passionate hobby-musician. Sergei was muscular with bulging biceps and a ripped torso that I could see through his flimsy t-shirt. He had a softness in his eyes that was revealing of his innocence and lack of guile.

He spoke no English but sent me many video recordings in which he had carefully choreographed his singing and guitar-playing in beautiful settings, including in the backdrop of snow-capped mountains, in front of a fireplace and walking through a flower garden. Before we parted ways, the teacher gave me fridge magnets from her city, Orenburg. Sergei wanted to give me something, anything, so he gave me his phone. I refused to accept it, but he assured me—with the English teacher translating for him—that this was a second phone he didn't use much, and he really wanted me to keep it to remember him by.

On another ride in a second-class coupé, I met two men from Omsk, both civil engineers, who refilled beer in soft drink bottles and drank through the journey, munching on chips, before going to sleep with deep, rhythmic snoring.

The next morning I had long conversations with them about their work projects, which they admitted were limited to Omsk and the surrounding regions. They hadn't travelled much within Russia, they said, not to Moscow in the west or Irkutsk in the east.

They did not seem curious, quite content where they were with what they had. This was refreshing. I wondered what it would be like to live with that level of contentment, an assuredness that you are not missing out. When you don't know that you are missing out, you are not missing out.

Of all these encounters, the strangest was the night I spent on a train with a Chihuahua. It is common for Russian women to carry pets in a basket on the train. I had the misfortune of spending twenty-six hours in a train coupe in close proximity to a beige Chihuahua that wouldn't stop staring at me. The pet parent, a woman in her thirties, took excessive care of the chihuahua, talking to him, opening the cage's window so that she could stroke his head, and feed him frequently.

For the entire journey, this dog did not take his eyes off me. It spooked me to such an extent that I could not sleep in peace even when the lights were out because I could feel the dog's eyes on me all the time. When I did fall asleep out of fatigue and opened my eyes, the first thing I saw was the dog's eyes boring into mine. I yelped and sat up, startled and irritated although all he did was stare. Even if the pet parent noticed it, she didn't let on that she knew how uncomfortable it made me.

Mid-morning, the dog got restless in his tiny cage and started to make a fuss. The cage was on the top berth and the woman stood on the lower berth to reach the cage and stroke her pet. She then opened the cage gate and within a split second, the dog ran out, first jumping to the other upper berth and then climbing his way down to the ground, getting lost between the suitcases under the seat.

All the passengers from the wagon, me included, joined forces to find the pet and put him back in the cage. It took fifteen excruciatingly long minutes with much shuffling about and screaming the pet's name, a guttural sound like Slorov or Krotov, that I couldn't get. I just made some noises, pretending to call out to the pet.

When the pet was found, the passengers celebrated with more tea and cookies while I sighed in relief as the pet continued to stare at me from inside the cage for the rest of the trip. Those were deep eyes that got under my skin. What did he want? I wish I knew. Two hours later, I stepped off, never happier to get off a train.

The oft-quoted metaphor for life describes it as a long bus journey where people get in and out at various stops.

Some people sit next to us, we have conversations, spend moments, share experiences, and make memories before they get off the bus at their stop. These memories, and the people who sit next to us on the bus ride of our life shape who we become, test our values and give us lessons to reflect upon.

No matter how torturous or enjoyable a journey, when our station arrives, we leave the people behind. It does not matter what stage we were at in our interaction, exchange, or relationship. And whether ready or not, we have to walk into the next experience that life has to offer.

Life's metaphor of the never-ending journey came alive for me over the span of one month in the world's longest train ride across Russia. I met strangers, exchanged thoughts, and we left each other a little changed before parting ways. At the end of every such brief relationship, I understood that the encounter was important, and how I felt while leaving was equally important.

It is said that the most spiritually aware beings are those who can enjoy an experience to its optimum level, and when it is time to leave, they let go with grace. Every person stays in our life, for however brief a moment, only for the time that is destined. During that time, many exchanges take place. We exchange words, thoughts, ideas, money, memories, and food. What remains is how we made the other person feel, and how the other person made us feel. It is the essence of why we move, travel, and interact.

Sometimes, the briefest of encounters can leave the deepest of impacts. When I travel, I expose myself to such possibilities. Some journeys are rich with encounters while others push me deeper within my own mind. It is this joy of the unknown that also makes travel a neverendingly joyous pursuit.

9

Embracing Carpe Diem from the Cool Air in Amsterdam

My alarm did not ring, but my trusty internal clock still woke me up just in time to catch the first train out of Paris to Amsterdam. I rushed to the Gare du Nord and had to sprint across the large hall to the platform. The train was waiting. Now I had to do another sprint to find my wagon. I had three minutes before the doors shut. Panting, I stopped to catch a breath.

Just as I was about to get on the train, three men in suits stopped me. They flashed their ID cards, which I didn't bother to look at in my nervousness. This was exactly as I had seen in the movies, but the experience of being stopped by an authority in a foreign country was nerve-wracking.

The man leading this small group asked me in English, with a strong French accent, 'Where are you going?'

'To Amsterdam on that train,' I said, pointing to the train, which I didn't want to miss. My heartbeat was faster than usual and I could feel my pulse quicken. I really didn't want to miss that train.

'We need to check your bag,' he said.

I didn't think I had a choice.

I had a small duffel bag and a handbag. One man checked my handbag while the other opened the front and back zippers of the duffel bag. He found the main zipper locked and asked me for the key. They're seriously doing this, I thought, and fished out the key from my handbag, handing it over with trembling hands. He checked every piece of clothing and the souvenirs I had bought from Paris.

The man put everything back in place and locked the bag.

'Thank you for your cooperation,' the man said.

'Was there a problem?' I asked, with just thirty seconds to go before the train doors shut. But I was also terribly curious about why they had stopped me.

'We were working on a tip, Ma'am. Have a nice day,' is all he said.

I rushed into the train and ten seconds later, the automatic doors shut. I slumped on the nearest seat out of sheer relief from making it in time. I waited for my heart rate to normalise and took deep breaths to calm down. These cops should time these random checks better, I thought, wondering what a mess I would be in if I had missed this connection.

I found my seat in a comfortable and mostly empty train that whizzed past the European countryside. Two friends from London, Sebastien and Nicholas, were driving from Brussels to Amsterdam. They planned to spend the day with me before I flew back to London the same evening. We had set a meeting point at a café in central Amsterdam.

I reached by 10 a.m. and they promptly arrived, too. Sebastien was a delight to be around. He truly lived in the moment, fully experiencing the present environment, and taking every sensory joy in it. He didn't take life seriously at all, which lent his energy an air of cloudy fluffiness. Nicholas was quiet with a gentle smile and ever-ready practical wisdom.

'Did you get it?' I asked Sebastien. He giggled like a schoolboy and pulled out the marijuana cigarette, which we had decided to try for the first time, and simply because we were allowed to try it in a coffeehouse in this country.

Sebastien had bought it off the counter at the café. We drank coffee and smoked with high expectations of extreme happiness and escape into a fantasy world.

'It tastes like dried leaves,' I said, almost spitting it out.

'What do you expect? It *is* dried leaves,' said Nicholas. We waited for some reaction. We hoped to see objects floating up, or people looking different. Nothing happened.

'Maybe it'll take a while longer. Let's drink some more coffee,' suggested Sebastien. So, we drank more coffee and waited.

'We are probably not meant to expect anything. Maybe we'll experience the lightness if we don't focus on it,' he said, and started to talk about other things. We laughed and joked about everything and nothing in particular. Still, we felt no change in mood or state of mind.

Nicholas shrugged and said, 'Well, maybe that's all there is to it. Let's go out and get some fresh air.'

We walked out of the café and to the car park. Sebastien stopped in his tracks. I stopped next to him and asked what happened. He pointed to the car and exclaimed: 'Look! My car!'

A yellow clamp was locked around the car's left front wheel. He had parked the car in a no-parking zone and was being fined for it. Sebastien was first struck by shock, and when the situation had sunk in, which took only a few seconds, he burst out laughing. He looked around and between loud laughter asked, 'What do we do now? How are we supposed to drive out of here?'

Nicholas and I joined Sebastien, responding to his uncontrolled laughter. Just then a cop walked up and asked Sebastien, 'Are you the owner of this vehicle, sir?'

'Yes. What do I do?' Sebastien asked between giggles.

The cop pulled out his receipt book and wrote down the car and violation details. 'That would be 80 Euros,' he said.

Sebastien said sure, and gleefully pulled out his wallet, handing over €80. The two men chit-chatted a while longer about the weather, the best hangout spots, and about the status of car parking violation collections in a day in this neighbourhood.

Sebastien was happy to continue the chatter, but Nicholas reminded him that it was time to leave. He shook hands with the cop and wished him a great day before we all got into the car and drove out of that street.

There was silence for a few minutes before Sebastien burst out laughing again. We joined him and laughed uncontrollably for a long time.

'Are you high?' I asked him.

'Not at all, but wasn't *that* funny?' he asked, still amused by the event.

'No, it wasn't that funny. You're high,' said Nicholas.

'No, guys, it's not the cigarette. I seriously thought it was funny. Here was a situation, which was not in our control. Whatever had to happen had already happened. There was no way I could reverse time and park the car elsewhere. There was only one option, which was to pay the fine. I had a total of €200 in my pocket and 80 went as contribution to the Amsterdam government. I could brood and worry about it, which still wouldn't change the situation. Or I could treat this like a fun experience, which would definitely keep my mood happy, weed or no weed. So, I chose happiness,' he explained in a logical sequence being coherent.

'You know you're a rare one, no?' Nicholas commented.

'Yes. Weird also,' he replied.

Two incidents took place in a span of a few hours that were not in our control: My random bag-checking at the train station in Paris, and Sebastien's brush with the traffic violation.

The response to each was different—I reacted with panic and fear of missing the train while Sebastien reacted with total acceptance of emptying out almost half his wallet. He chose happiness over worry. He understood and practiced happiness as a choice, and this is the best form of spirituality there is out there.

I had renewed respect for Sebastien after this incident. He had shown through example that in every situation, we are still in control even though it may seem as though we are not in charge. We are always in charge of how we react to a situation or a life experience.

Accepting and surrendering to the moment may seem like a weak response when all we want to do is fight for what we want. It takes immense courage to let things go, especially those things that we love and are important to us. Surrendering does not mean that we accept defeat and not fight at all for what we want and what is important. But we should be able to pick carefully the battles worth fighting for.

We spent the rest of the day roaming the streets, walking by only a few of its 165 beautiful canals, and clicking photos by only a few of its 80 quaint bridges in central Amsterdam. The city has 1,281 bridges.

Amsterdam stands on 11 million wooden poles sunk into the sand. Over time, some of the poles holding up a building sink further, tilting the building to one side. We saw some of the slanting houses. And then, we saw bicycles everywhere. It is said that there are 1.9 bicycles for every person in Amsterdam. As of 2023, Amsterdam has 11.5 lakh residents. You do the math for the possible number of bicycles in this city of canals.

We also learnt that the Amsterdam municipality runs a special bicycle salvaging department that uses boats to which are attached metal claws that scrape the bottoms of canals to dredge up about 25,000 bicycles from the water every year.

How do so many cycles end up in the canals? There are a variety of reasons—some just fall into the canal by accident while riding or parking close to the edge of the water. Some others are deliberately thrown into the water by petty mischief-makers for cheap thrills, and then there are some other cycles that are abandoned in the canal waters by owners who don't want to take their cycles all the way to the dump yard. Armed with these facts, I saw the canals and the cycles in a new light.

We ate ice-cream and walked by the sex trade shops. Some of the women in the shop windows waved at us and we waved back. We lay on the grass and took in the city's clean air.

For all the hype around it, marijuana may not have affected the quality of a day well spent in Amsterdam, but it was still an experience to be savoured—just because you are allowed to.

The city, on the other hand, had an easy-going quality to it that enriched our experience manifold. With its cheerful vibe, Amsterdam enabled us friends to dip into our own reserves of happiness.

What I most enjoyed, though, was the company of Sebastien and Nicholas. To anyone who meets Sebastien for the first time, he may appear scattered and superficial. But he lives in the moment and cherishes every relationship irrespective of what he can get out of it. He takes everything beyond the transactional without needing to be deeply serious about it. In a way, his personality mirrored the ease of Amsterdam that we found joy in, a city that follows the live-and-let-live policy.

Even after many years, Sebastien is the kind of friend who sends Christmas postcards. He has kept me updated on his life, kids, and work. In every family photo, he looks radiant, ready to burst out of the postcard in laughter and joy.

And the most important of them all—when it is time to say goodbye, he does so with grace. He knows that the next moment is ready and waiting to be experienced.

I LOVE

Some places have the power to stir desire, bringing up the most sensuous parts of the human experience. I travel in search of these experiences to test the full power of how much the heart can hold.

10

Submitting to a Brief Love Affair in Barcelona

Barcelona understands transience like no other city in the world. The city loves the promise of tomorrow, but it really lives for the emotion of the moment. It is a city of fly-by-night visitors who fascinate about time's ephemerality. Being in Barcelona was like meeting a city for an intimate, deep conversation about life and how to navigate her curves and surprises. You be the one to spring a surprise, Barcelona was telling me.

Barcelona is not in a hurry, as is New York or Mumbai, where speed determines survival; nor is it like Rome or Berlin, where the baggage of history weighs like heavy chains around the ankles.

Catalonia's cry for independence from Spain is visible from the locals' insistence on speaking only Catalan and to treat every football match against Madrid as war, no less. But Barcelona doesn't let this activism spoil the mood of the moment. Whatever is important is all happening right now, the city was showing me. She showed me how to live for this present moment, how to live for the now and how to make it come alive for you.

For the people of this poetic land, time is sliced into short spurts of deep emotional engagement—a spirited public art project, a mercurial football game, an imaginative night out at the theatre, and a passionate one-night stand.

Barcelona is all about zest. It's about giving a moment all you've got, investing every emotion at your disposal. It doesn't matter who stirs your pot of pleasure, or where and under what circumstances.

A friend described Barcelona as a place where barons and fishermen meet at the bar, and you wouldn't be able to tell one from the other. The well-heeled and the down-at-heel rub shoulders across this city, which has its soul trapped in a sad love story, which is now bursting with art and expression at every corner, in a cry of agony over a lover who escaped through the torn tapestry of time.

Barcelona wears a sundress and leather boots with fringes and would embrace you even if you turned up wearing a buttoned-down shirt and dress pants. But she would tell you to roll up your sleeves and un-tuck your shirt.

The city cares less about grand symbols and prefers to wear her heart on her sleeve. Barcelona could have hosted the Eiffel Tower, but the discerning town rejected Eiffel's design and embraced Antoni Gaudi, making room for colourfully quirky art and the celebrity architect's idiosyncrasies. Paris took the Eiffel Tower, but Barcelona entered a long-term romance with Gaudi's architecture; the diamond ring sealing this commitment is the La Sagrada Familia.

I stood on the grounds of this iconic Roman Catholic Church that has been in construction for over 135 years and couldn't help but see the cathedral as a mud castle of magnanimous proportions. Its spiky bell towers and twisting columns were the stuff of untethered imagination. World tourists flocked to this giant construction site, not minding the workers, cranes, rubble, and drilling noise, to see Gaudi's vision at play. It was not yet a cathedral, but it held the promise of being one someday. Barcelona isn't fussed about the cathedral's completion. The city is in love with the idea of a never-ending game of guessing just what Gaudi's design intentions were for this mega monument of worship.

Gaudi's architecture is what made me travel to Barcelona. But being in the city was like meeting a teacher who would show me how to feel with all my heart. Barcelona did not disappoint. With every passing hour, she was unravelling a bit more of herself. In turn, those rich insights were, unknowingly at the time, adding nuance to my life's philosophy.

Take Gaudi's architecture, for example. I had never seen buildings so bendy and flowy in such an organic and colourfully mosaic form. I tried to imagine Gaudi's motivation for his designs: If there's anything straight, try to curve it and see if the building stands this artistic innovation.

The technical term is Catalan Modernism—if you've imagined it, Gaudi has already probably designed a building out of it somewhere. Gaudi's art is telling of his disdain for all things straight-laced and prissy. His protest was dramatic and many-hued. In Barcelona, he had found the right home for his theatre of the absurd.

The city was showing me, first of all, what it's like to be unabashedly creative. She was then showing me how to be creative within a structure. Sure, Gaudi's architecture is all bendy, seemingly defying order and tradition. But look at how much fun it is to add colour and creativity to a bare frame.

I asked myself what this looks like in life and relationships. Make your own rules. Experiment. Think. Think again. Question what you think you know. Barcelona was giving me all these invaluable nuggets by simply giving me access to her spirit.

Gaudi's unmistakable imprint on the city of Barcelona ran through its streets, spilling over to the city's veins and creating a hipster vibe. But this was the hipster that started trends rather than follow them.

The world knows La Sagrada Familia as the object of Gaudi's obsession through the last years of his life leading up to his accidental death in 1926 (he was hit by a tram and didn't get medical attention on time). The architect's love affair with Barcelona started with Casa Vicens, which he built for a realtor in 1885.

Now standing as a house museum in the Gracia neighbourhood, Casa Vicens was that first handshake between Gaudi and the city. The house has mosaic tiles in palm leaf design at the entrance, cast iron gates, and a compatible marriage of exterior and interior through ceramics, painting, and murals—the city had never seen anything like it before; it was love at first sight.

Walking on the terrace of this gorgeous house and looking out into the quiet Spanish neighbourhood, I felt at peace. The Mediterranean sunshine felt warm on my cheeks, the cool breeze balanced the heat of a sunny day, and the tower and dome on the terrace stirred a deep corner of my heart giving me a sense of belonging.

I marvelled at how Gaudi had elevated the stature of nature in architecture. We typically disturb nature while making more room for our homes and buildings. Gaudi was showing that, while at it, we can still salute nature that was here before us. We are only visitors, he was saying.

I lingered in the house just long enough to see everything and left even though I wanted to soak in the emotions that were triggered. It was a strange mix of being uncomfortable in the comfortable. I was aware of it and didn't want to indulge this paradox too much.

Peeling away from Gaudi's architecture that dotted the streets, I opened up to the other sensual experiences that Barcelona had to offer. I visited the La Boqueria indoor market and walked the aisles, appreciating the visual treat of bright-coloured fruits and vegetables stacked up in perfect pyramids. For a taste of the city's dark side, I popped in at the Museu de Carrosses Fúnebres, one of the world's oldest shops and museums dedicated to magic, located in the Montjuic Cemetery.

I walked by the Magic Fountain of Montjuic as well as La Rambla, the pedestrian street bursting with wild colours and life. I popped in at the Picasso Museum, and walked past the beautifully designed El Quatre Gats, that famous haunt for Modernista artists like Picasso and Gaudi. It's said that Picasso hated Gaudi so much that he once said, 'Send Gaudi and the Sagrada Familia to hell!'

Simply walking on those streets, the city was teaching me to be bravely myself, even if some people find it too much. So what if you are too much? Be bravely so, Barcelona was telling me. She was also telling that only those worthy of a lot will eventually find you and align with you. This is the way, after all, that the city had attracted only those who dared to be themselves.

I saw more breathtaking architecture in the charming Gothic Quarter, and continued this sensual experience at La Barceloneta, a seaside neighbourhood with al-fresco restaurants lining the beachside. I was particularly interested in visiting the nudist beach, San Sebastian.

As I found a quiet spot on the beach and settled down to enjoy the waves, the day's walking caught up with me and I fell asleep. When I opened my eyes, I saw an old woman in her sixties lying a few feet to my right. She had taken off her bikini top to sunbathe. It took me a while to realise that I was staring at her; it took me longer to realise that my eyebrows were raised, my jaw had dropped, and my lips were parted. I collected myself and looked away. To my left, I saw a woman in her twenties, standing topless, staring at the water.

Visiting a nudist beach was on my list of things to do—it wasn't very high up the list, but it was there, nevertheless. I was excited to just be there and look around. I tried to act cool and uncaring by wearing sunglasses and casually looking around, when, in fact, I was checking them out—the men *and* the women!

When the novelty of the idea wore out, which didn't take too long, I decided to walk along the beach to my seaside hotel. I had an honest chat with myself on the walk back and decided that nudist beaches were not a big deal. Of course, there is high potential for excitability when nakedness is so brazenly strut about, but it all eventually calms down in the face of abundance.

Yet again, Barcelona was being herself, and was urging me to be me and not anyone else. Conform only if it feels right to you; only if it pleases you, she was saying.

I reached my hotel and sank into the lobby sofa, awaiting my turn to check e-mail on the hotel computer; those were the days of internet cafes.

'*Aap kaise ho* (How are you)?' a male voice with a clear American accent caught my attention. That was the only Hindi this young man knew, but it was enough to start a conversation that extended into the long night.

We walked the length of the beach and stole moments of tenderness under the half-moon. It was poetic justice that a short-lived romance should make itself available to me in this city. I lived the city's vibe for a day, and she rewarded me with an authentic experience that let me wade in the promise of desire, of being wanted and held, without conditions or contracts.

By the time I returned to my room just before dawn, Barcelona had gifted me a brief glimpse into her transience, including lessons in leaving behind, saying goodbye, and letting go—because only then was the next adventure going to present itself.

Love with all you've got. Hate, also, with all you've got. Do anything with all your heart. And when it is time to let go, let it all go, too, with all your heart.

As I took the flight back home, I knew that I was ready for another new experience. After all, love is a work in progress. All we have got to do is keep walking, even if it took forever. But who's keeping the time, anyway? Barcelona had taught me well.

11

Napoli's World-Famous Pizza Shows off Campanian Pizzazz

I had been in London three months and decided to gift myself a trip to Italy for my birthday. The idea seemed audacious for a young Indian student on her first time overseas. But my desire to travel outweighed the apprehensions, doubts, and fears of everything that could go wrong with a girl out and about in the big bad world.

I didn't believe in easing into Europe before taking this humongous leap. No exploring the English countryside or making a trip to nearby Scotland first. No. I was going to fly halfway across Europe to Italy. It was decided.

Why Italy? One word. Pizza. I was going to eat at the pizzeria rated as the best in the world. The L'Antica Pizzeria da Michele is still considered to be the best since it opened its doors in 1906. I wanted to taste pizza, truly, for what it is supposed to be.

The first time with anything, whether it is taking a flight or setting out to ride a bike on your own, is always memorable. This first overseas holiday gave me a storehouse of memories not just in that first bite into the luscious pizza slice but also in every emotion, big and small. I had never felt as alive as I had on this trip to Italy. Every sensation was amplified in its uniqueness. Little did I realise at the time that I was tasting the freedom of the road, the eternal lure of travel. I also did not know then that I was never going to be the same again, and I was never going to look at travel the same way ever again.

From applying for a visa appointment to getting the papers ready to finally seeing the visa stamped on my passport, every step of the way was a victory worth celebrating. I was doing every small and big job alone. This time of my life was telling me that I was capable of all this and anything that I pleased to do.

On the night before my five-day trip, I could barely sleep. It was hard to contain the excitement. I planned to take the Tube to the airport, which meant that I had to leave in the early morning hours, as early as 4 a.m., when the roads would be still and dark. I dragged my bag across the empty streets, the duffel's wheels echoing through the alleys.

I reached King's Cross station, which was bustling with activity. I had crossed another hurdle. Every step of this journey was akin to smashing the barriers that came in the way of courage. Each small step added a bit more weight to my confidence.

In a new place when everything was unfamiliar, the only way to survive was to breathe deeply and take one step at a time. When I had done it successfully once, I knew that I would get bolder to again cross the invisible threshold of courage. And so it was. It is the reason why the first experience is always considered special. The first time will never come again.

When I landed at the Leonardo da Vinci-Fiumicino airport in Rome, I was pleasantly surprised and quite thrilled with the noise and chaos. Passengers spoke loudly with abandon and not in the cautious, reserved manner that I was now used to seeing in most of London. Also, people lay on the floor, and there was a more laidback, devil-may-care atmosphere than in the UK.

The city was everything I expected it to be, and more. The cobbled streets, the architecture, art, fashion, and even River Tiber that flowed silently in the middle of the city, exuded the bittersweet mix of Rome's turbulent history. Rome was a living museum and everywhere I turned, I spotted a work of art. Not just the sculptures and the deliberately crafted things of beauty, every item in a public place, whether a street-side bench or a post office building, provoked strong emotions.

The plazas at the crossroads displayed works of art that were capable of stimulating love, longing, desire, aspiration, lust, sorrow, and calm—either one at a time or several emotions together at once.

Three days in Rome was a bit of a rush, but I managed to see the artworks of the greats, walked in the Vatican, mailed a postcard back to my home in London from the Vatican Post Office, attended Mass one evening, and stared at the Sistine Chapel's ceiling till I was asked to please leave. I touched the broken walls of the Colosseum, shuddering at the thought of the gladiator fights there.

I threw a coin in the Trevi Fountain, with a fervent wish to return to this great city. I sat for a couple of hours, listening to the soothing gush of water mixed with the chaotic drone of tourists while admiring the sculptures' beauty. Even the water seemed to flow with a quiet reverence for the art it was allowed to dance on.

One online review of the Trevi Fountain dubbed it overrated. It was a rather irresponsible comment, considering that the city's oldest source of water—from the Aqua Virgo Aqueduct in 19 BC—stands eighty-five feet tall. Yes, it spills a whopping 2.8 million cubic feet of water every day (that's 4.3 million buckets!) but the fountain also gives back through charity. The fountain bed collects about 3,000 Euros every day, thanks to the wish-making ritual of throwing a coin in. These coins are collected and given to the needy through a supermarket programme.

Tourists flocked to the fountain's edge to click pictures and throw coins while perpetuating an urban tourist ritual as well as a social cause.

Unperturbed by the crowds or its judgment, I watched a middle-aged woman hold a long, expandable metal rod and patiently dip it into the water, the bottom of which was a thick bed of coins. The magnet at the end of the rod collected one coin at a time, which she dropped in her bag.

Tourists looked at her with raised eyebrows, but she didn't care. This was a woman with attitude and focus, and she perhaps knew well that what she did was illegal. Only three years prior, in 2002, a thief who stole coins from the Trevi Fountain for thirty-four years was finally caught. With so much chequered history and Baroque magic in the fountain, how could it be overrated? I found this fountain to be an urban legend.

I was in awe not just with what I witnessed around me but also with what was happening inside me. The water in my cup of emotions was being splashed about vigorously as every new exposure poured life into my being. Isn't that what travel is supposed to do?

I ticked on my list every must-see place in Rome. And I ate pizza at the popular spots listed as local favourites. The Italians spoke too loudly, the restaurants were too crowded, the pizzas were too large, and the cheese was too greasy. But every Margherita pizza that I ate during my travels in Italy was like savouring a work of art.

I was going to taste the Mona Lisa of all pizzas at the birthplace of this great, now-cosmopolitan food. I took a train to Naples. I had read about a pizza place just outside the railway station as being the original and best.

I went there, a tad early for lunch, but the restaurant was crowded. A rotund waiter with a thick moustache and serious demeanour led me to the basement. It was empty; I was the only customer there. I ordered the classic Margherita pizza again. It was too large, but this was their smallest size.

In the quiet of the basement with empty tables and chairs all around me, the waiter stood unblinking, staring at me expressionless while I ate. When I enjoy food, I make loud smacking noises, and here with the best pizza in the world on the table before me, I wasn't going to be bothered about etiquette, especially in an empty dining room. The waiter stared and watched me relish my pizza to the last delicious slice. Satiated, I told myself that I would burn the calories with all the walking.

Still expressionless, the waiter brought me the cheque. When I paid and left, he was still looking at me, with not even a hint of a smile. As I headed out, I caught the blackboard on which was scrawled in English the recipe for the famous Napoli pizza. The main ingredient, it read, was the water in Naples. Without the water, the pizza just wouldn't taste as good anywhere else in the world!

I walked around in the tiny town, unremarkable when compared to the history that, say a city like Rome carries on its shoulders, but still beautiful as any quaint European town. When I had worked up an appetite again, I walked to the L'Antica Pizzeria da Michele, a charming as ever café-style pizzeria rated as the best in the world. The hospitality was far warmer here, and it was a clear tourist trap. The place was buzzing with excitement. I could hear tongues from all parts of the world.

And how was the pizza? I will be honest. I could not tell the difference between this pizza and the one I had eaten only a few hours earlier. It still tasted as divine. However, there was a difference between Napoli pizza and the ones I ate elsewhere in Italy. The dough was crisper and the toppings were fresher with the juiciest tomato slices. The cheese was also a bit more on the slithery texture.

My conclusion is that just as it is difficult to get a bad Mysore masala dosa in any part of Mysore, it is as difficult to get a badly baked pizza in any part of Italy. For the touch of difference in the Napoli pizza, I tend to agree with the recipe on the blackboard. The water in Naples makes all the difference.

I am no foodie nor does every type of food excite me. I consider food to be nourishing and healing. It has the power to talk to the body, give it the nourishment it needs and fix what needs to be fixed. Italian food has an emotional touch point unlike little else in the world. It has travelled the world and penetrated various world cultures.

Pizza is a comforting sight on every menu card in any part of the world. Its staying power is in its hold over our emotions. And it is this magnetic pull that had me obsessively plan my first overseas trip from London to Italy in search of the best pizza. The two pizza experiences at Napoli, although starkly different in ambience and similar in taste, had fulfilled me emotionally. It brought to life a part of my heart that wanted to remain curious while continuing to seek out such unique experiences. For this, I will always be grateful to Italy, and specifically to the Napoli pizza.

Digging Up The Past In Pompeii

Food was not the only way in which Italy was stirring my pot of emotions. I will always remember Italy as the country where I had my first experience of working my way through a metal turnstiles barricade.

I met Taree Booth, a backpacker from Australia, and we decided to travel to Pompeii together. We bought tickets at the train station counter and dashed towards the platforms to take the earliest train out but I got stuck at the turnstile.

The machine ate up my ticket but wouldn't move the steel rods a second time to let me out. The truth is I had turned the turnstile once while still staying on one side of the machine. The complete truth is that I had turned the turnstile once to see how it works, and to ensure that I wouldn't get stuck between the metal rods.

It was the first time I had encountered this kind of technology. I had never seen anything like it in India. Three rods stuck out like a robot's arms that would crush you if it decided not to like you. The thought was terrifying. Who knows what might happen if I forced the rods to turn against their will! So I stood and turned it slowly once for practice. And then it wouldn't give me a second chance. I knew this machine was all sorts of evil.

Taree had used the adjacent gate and was on the other side urging me to get another ticket and rush. The train was about to leave. I asked her to run, and that I would follow her on the next train. She left while I waited in the station, observing passengers move past the turnstile with utter lack of respect for it. I should probably ignore it, too, I thought.

When it was time for me to cross those metal rods again, I did as I had watched the others do. It was easy enough, and I felt a small sense of achievement. I didn't want those turnstiles to ever come to India but they're everywhere these days. Years later, I got stuck again at New York with a slightly modified version. I was still terrified but I could mask it well this time.

My misadventure with the turnstiles undid the travel plans with Taree as I could not find her. It was not the cell phone era yet. I was gifted another solo day.

My intention of visiting Pompeii was to travel back in time and encounter a slice of history that was frozen on this large tract of land.

I hired an audio guide and listened to dramatised stories of the devastation caused in Pompeii when Mount Vesuvius erupted in 79 AD. I walked the streets of what was once a thriving Roman city, buried in metres of thick volcanic ash. The city was found to be almost intact when it was discovered in the mid-1700s and was excavated.

Across the archaeological site, I saw the plaster casts of humans and animals that were buried under ash. Once the organic parts of a body were decayed, plaster was poured into the body cavities. Such plaster casts were laid all over the archaeological site to determine what life looked like in those last moments before the tragedy. The paved roads of Pompeii were perfectly straight. It was an old city site, preserved almost intact.

When dipping into memories, whether personal or the preserved history of a culture or civilisation, we can be completely authentic only when we allow all the shades of memories and emotions to emerge. There are happy and sad memories, there are playful and horrifying ones, and there are also pleasant and nasty memories. To truly sit with the past entails sitting with everything that the mind throws up.

The walk through the ancient city of Pompeii enabled me to forget myself in the stories of another age when I could see before my eyes the lives they possibly led. The audio narration added music and drama to history. It made me think of how I look back at my own memories.

Do I filter them based on how I want to remember an episode from the past? Or do I sit in all honesty with an open mind to accept memories of every shade, whether I like them or not? I realised that I do the former.

As the sun set on Pompeii, I walked the cobbled streets and wondered if it is necessary to remember things just as they happened. The human mind is naturally designed to alter memories with the passage of time. Do we then really remember events as they exactly happened? Likely not. Then what becomes most important when thinking of the past?

Am I fooling myself if I am erasing traumatic memories to survive? Is that so bad? But then, doesn't the trauma make me who I am? I tussled with this debate for a long time as I walked in silence looking at so much history all around me.

The preserved history in Pompeii showed me that the stories (whether remembered to exacting standards or not) that we tell ourselves and others matter the most. Does the story heal a part of us? Is the story teaching us something about the human condition? Is it telling us how to deal with greed, envy, lust, and anger? Is it teaching us empathy? If it is not doing any of this, then what good is a story?

Carrying this reflective take on stories from the past and our memories, I headed back to Rome. This time, I experienced the infamous tardiness of Italian trains. What should have been a three-hour ride took five hours. Children cried, parents grew impatient, people snored and talked too loudly. This social chatter was a welcome break from my time alone reflecting.

Then I saw how stories can be simply entertaining, too. They can offer relief from the heaviness of our daily struggles. They can soothe, they can pamper, and they can be the much-needed breath of fresh air.

A Tower Leans In

Italy had so much more to offer from its box of emotions. The next morning, I took a day trip to Pisa. This trip was slow-paced, and I had some time to enjoy the Italian countryside. I climbed up the winding stairs of the tower and experienced the slant, tilting heavier with each floor.

On the topmost floor, with the tilt at six degrees or 13 feet off the perpendicular on the south side, the feeling truly was that of the ground beneath your feet slanting too dangerously. I had to hold on tight to the railings. Then, I asked myself what our fascination could be with a building that is about to fall off when there are marvellous structures that surpass human ingenuity? Is it perhaps because it hasn't toppled yet? And we want to see it as it tilts?

This 12th century magnificent miracle started to tilt almost immediately after it was constructed. It is the cathedral's bell tower at Pisa, with seven bells to represent the seven musical notes. Today, the leaning bell tower is, understandably, more popular than the cathedral.

Back on the ground, as I aimlessly walked the streets, I sensed Tuscany's assured and self-confident vibe. I walked off the tourist path into a residential neighbourhood. An aged woman was pushing a bicycle, in no hurry to reach her destination.

She looked dapper in a dress, a scarf tied over her head, and wearing dark sunglasses. She didn't speak English, but she understood when I pointed to my camera and asked if I could click her photo. She agreed and posed with her cycle in front of a beautiful marble statue of an Italian man.

This click remains one of my favourite images from Italy. It was not the Sistine Chapel, not the Colosseum, and not even a close-up of the world's best pizza. It was the picture of a woman who was going about her day on her cycle and had the patience and the heart to oblige a random tourist that she will never again see. There was not a trace of irritation on her face. She was going with the flow, her wrinkles telling the story of days that she continues to embrace and a life that she is learning to conquer.

We sat on a bench in companionable silence, smiling at each other when our eyes met. Her smile ended up being my best return gift to keep in my heart for as long as my memory is on my side. We were two women from different parts of the world who didn't need words to communicate. The years she carried on her shoulders told me that she was winning in her own way.

As for me, my trip to Italy was a personal victory. I will always reflect on my first overseas solo trip with pride and love of self. I didn't feel lonely at any point, nor did I crave company. If I found people to talk to, I was happy to engage in conversation. If not, I was happy to soak in the rich atmosphere. My senses were fully alive and my instincts were alert. I plunged into the experience, which was the only way it should have been. In that, Italy was a great teacher.

12

Mesmerised by Montmartre, Mona Lisa, and Marie Antoinette's Love Shack

The last of the sun's rays faded and the streetlights spilled a pool of yellow light on the ground around the lamp posts. A woman spotted her lover in the oncoming traffic of pedestrians and dashed straight into his waiting arms. He held the small of her back urgently and leaned in to vent all his love in a back-bending, deep passionate kiss.

He wrapped one arm around her waist, while the other was stretched out mid-air, holding up a large bouquet of fresh wild-red roses. Her white see-through dress clung to her curves and had a deep opening at her chest to reveal ample cleavage. Her hips were perked up by two-inch pointed-toe red stilettos, and her open wavy waist-length black hair was telling of her unbridled yearning. His dark grey suit, whiff of strong cologne and perfectly coiffed hair displayed similar intentions for an evening full of possibilities.

Right there, the French kiss, the romance of Paris came alive before my eyes on a busy street at twilight. That instant, so evocative of the famous World War Two photograph of a sailor kissing a uniformed nurse at Times Square, New York, froze in time as the world walked by. In that moment of intense passion, the sensuous beauty and magic of Paris burst forth.

This is the city where love is splayed out uninhibited—lovers kiss on the metro, under the tree, by the lamp post, on the pavement, at restaurants, in front of the Eiffel Tower, on top of the Eiffel Tower, on the grass, at doorways and in airports. Here, emotions are not suppressed but expressed without holding back—a true delight for any artist. It also explains why the entire city is like a painting in motion, blending and fusing emotions in creativity.

My first visit was to that temple of emotional expression, the Louvre, the world's largest art museum, to pay my respects to the most prevailing of artworks in modern times—the Mona Lisa. Navigating long queues to get a ticket, I chose a thematic self-guided tour and set off below that famous glass and steel pyramid to explore the Louvre on my own.

Dodging large groups of noisy tourists, I often found a quiet place from which to let these art treasures talk to me. When tourists milled about the Venus de Milo sculpture, the gleaming white larger-than-life size sculpture of female beauty, for example, I would stand away in a corner, opening up to her emotions and being vulnerable to her sensuality.

Art has a way of reaching into the deep recesses of the soul to pluck at often unfamiliar, and sometimes uncomfortable, feelings. I allowed the artworks this intrusion into my heart.

The Raft of the Medusa painting drove right through my open heart, wading in the chaos inside, its depiction of a shipwreck connecting with my deepest fears and anxieties. The Grande Odalisque was another painting in which the eyes of the naked woman holding a fan of peacock feathers bore into my soul, recognising me from eternity. I shuddered. As I made my way through room after room of fine art, my own emotions joined the ebb and flow of an ocean tide carrying the waves of life, death, and everything in between, emanating from these paintings.

When it was finally time to see the Mona Lisa, the viewing was surrounded by an aura of mystery, much like the painting itself. The painting was displayed in an isolated, climate-controlled room under dim lighting. Barricades kept visitors many feet away from the bulletproof glass case she was in. Yes, bulletproof. Now, who would carry a gun and make it this far into the museum through the multiple layers of security screening, I wondered? But before that, why would anyone want to shoot at a painting? Turns out, the smiling lady had been through quite a few adventures over the decades.

In 1911, a Louvre staffer hid over the weekend in the museum's supplies closet and waited till Monday morning, the day off at the museum, before walking out with the Mona Lisa under his smock. France and the world went into shock and mourned her disappearance by sending flowers and postcards in the lady's remembrance.

Pablo Picasso, then not yet famous, was falsely arrested as he was in possession of some Iberian sculptures that were earlier stolen from the Louvre. Picasso was found to be innocent and was released. The real thief was an Italian patriot who took the painting because he believed that Mona Lisa belonged to Italy, Da Vinci's home, and not France. He kept the painting in his apartment for two years before he was caught trying to sell it.

In 1956, one Ugo Ungaza threw a stone at the painting and damaged it near the lady's left elbow. The French government wasn't willing to take any more chances and built a room, estimated to have cost $7 million, and put away the painting in a bulletproof case.

France feels justified in offering this excessive protection for the lady, for in 2009, an angry Russian woman hurled a ceramic mug at the Mona Lisa, which the bulletproof glass successfully rebuffed. The attacker was angry because France rejected her citizenship application and wanted to vent.

In 1910, a man shot himself in front of the Mona Lisa painting. This makes stronger the case for bulletproof glass for the lady.

The room where the Mona Lisa was exhibited was flanked by watchful security guards, whose main job was to keep a close eye on the visitors. When I entered the room, about fifty visitors jostled for space, pushing and elbowing each other. Western society's ostensible claim to civility crumbled to the floor here as visitors from every nationality and culture resorted to a push here and a tug there to get a clear view of the Mona Lisa.

I stood for a few minutes patiently awaiting my turn. It clearly wasn't working, so I jumped right in and jostled my way to the front. At my first glimpse of the Mona Lisa, my exact thought was: *That's it*? At thirty by twenty-one inches, she was so small. The world's most famous woman had disappointed me in size. I stared at the tiny painting in a too-big muted-golden frame, covered in a giant glass case against a large blank wall.

Here was a woman who had inspired love and longing, irrespective of social stature. French emperor Napoleon hung the Mona Lisa painting on his bedroom wall for four years in the early 1800s, and then fell in love with a lookalike Italian descendant of the Mona Lisa, real name Lisa Gherardini.

In 1852, a man jumped from the fourth floor of a hotel balcony in Paris with this suicide note. 'For years, I have grappled desperately with her smile. I prefer to die.'

I stood for a few long minutes, observing the other visitors standing near me. Despite large signboards screaming that no photography was allowed inside the 'Mona Lisa Room', visitors delighted in trying to hoodwink the security guards' hawk eyes to click a quick picture of Mona Lisa in the glass case.

The year was 2006, when box digital cameras were common. Guards were posted in the room for the express purpose of preventing photography in the room. The result was awkward. A visitor would casually lift the camera and a booming voice from one end of the room would shout: 'No photos, please!' The visitors seemed to care more about getting a photo than actually looking at the Mona Lisa.

I had had enough and walked out. I blamed the other paintings on which I had expended so much energy, my emotions so rabble-roused that I was exhausted, with nothing more left to give to the most iconic half-smirking woman in a frame.

Feet tired from the walking and soul tired from the sentimental rough and tumble, I left the museum into the nippy evening air to allow air, food, and wine to replenish my spent energy.

So much drama around a work of art! Isn't art supposed to take us into our own hearts, making us test the extent of what we can feel? Instead, here I was, staring at a world-famous painting of unremarkable size shielded by layers over multiple layers of security so that we stay occupied with the fuss *around* her rather than allow her eyes and her half-smile to sway us.

When I thought about it some more, I wondered if a long-distance romance with Mona Lisa was more alluring than actually seeing her at the Louvre. When I saw the Mona Lisa in a photograph on my phone or as an A4-size printed poster in my local neighbourhood café, she brought a stillness to my world. 'Stop. Look at me,' she said with a commanding voice.

I expected such a personal touch to be amplified at the museum where I would meet the original. I expected to feel her aura fill up the room and reach some unknown part of my heart that was waiting to be stirred awake to a new sensation. Alas, it was not to be. And this was the disappointment. It made me wonder if I was better off imagining the Mona Lisa aura rather than trying to experience it first-hand.

I will admit, every time I look at the Mona Lisa today, I carry the slightest disappointment along with the appreciation for such a stunning creation that came from an artist's imagination and talent.

France had more to offer. It was a storehouse of emotions that it didn't hide away in boxes kept in the dark. France was the unabashed lover whose feelings bled out into the open without any shame or regret. I decided to roll in France's potpourri of sentiments.

Over the next few days, I roamed the streets of Montmartre, dipping into this hip neighbourhood's checkered past and uncertain future. I climbed the steps of Sacré-Cœur Basilica twice to take in the views, aimlessly strolled the cobblestone streets, wondering if I was stepping on the same stones that famous artists like Monet, Van Gogh, Picasso, and Dali must have once walked on. I stumbled upon the Les Deux Moulins, the two windmills, experienced the Moulin Rouge, peeped into the Montmartre Cemetery, and ate a deliciously baked crepe.

Heading towards the Seine River, I spent an entire afternoon people-watching and waving to the cruise boats that floated by. I was ready to experience another icon of Paris, the 'Lady of Paris' that watches over the city like a parent, the Notre Dame Cathedral.

As with most world-famous tourist attractions, it was difficult to get a photograph of the cathedral without strangers in it, so I didn't try. Putting the camera away, I craned my neck to consume its intricate French Gothic architecture with its giant arches and ribbed vaults. The structure was a glorious web of domes, holding up walls and windows, and flying buttresses that curved high up in the air to support taller parts of the structure. The grand spire was equally stunning.

When I entered the cathedral's main hall, a settling calm descended over me. The steady hum of tourists notwithstanding, my emotions that were stirred at the Louvre were now stilling. The rich and bright-coloured stained-glass windows inspired wonderment, and when I touched the walls and pillars that had heard countless prayers over 850 years, a tear escaped my eye. This cathedral was definitely a woman, for only she can carry in her bosom the weight of the world and still invite the devout to rest in her open arms.

I took the 422 steps from the North Tower to get a closer look at the gargoyles that guard this Lady of Paris and keep watch over the city. I tried to count the steps on my way up, but then lost my concentration when an American man started a conversation with me. I tried to do the same on my way down but felt dizzy trying to keep up. I'll have to take their word for it on the exact number of steps.

On my last full day in Paris, I took a day picnic to Versailles to soak in the opulence of French history. Following the advice of local bartenders and tour guides, I reached early and skipped the typically long lines to get into the large palace of 700 rooms, 67 staircases, and 1,200 fireplaces.

My first stop was to the Hall of Mirrors, the historic room where the Peace Treaty was signed between

Germany and the Allies to formally end the First World War. It was full of gold sculptures, crystal chandeliers, an arched ceiling covered with artwork, and mirrors on any leftover space on the walls pouring out this flamboyance manifold.

The Grand Trianon is a relief from the overflowing flashiness throughout the palace. Tucked away in a quiet corner, this room shines in understated elegance and dignity. The Petit Trianon, which came to be called Marie Antoinette's Estate, was built by King Louis the thirteenth for his mistress.

An unimaginative rectangular building, this was a getaway for royalty from their excessive formality of court life. This mistress's den was later gifted to Queen Marie Antoinette by King Louis the fourteenth, who used it as a love shack and a place for relaxation with minimal intervention by servants.

See what I said earlier about the classic French openness about their passions? Emotions are meant to be expressed, not to be shut out from the world. And no matter how you feel, there is no room for carrying any shame about them. Every aspect of French society reflects this desire for expression.

I saw it also in the never-ending gardens in Versailles, where I spent the better part of the day roaming the manicured lawns, admiring the perfectly cropped bushes, the bright-coloured flowers in full bloom and the many elaborate fountains, many of them in gold!

In my few hours in Versailles, it was impossible for me to see all the 253 statues and 55 fountains, but I did walk past several of them to get a sense of the grandeur of the place. Talk about being too much. One has got to love it when in France!

A brochure about the gardens said that about 2 lakh trees and 2.1 lakh flowering plants are planted every year in these gardens.

I sat on the ornately beautiful benches and imagined being a part of the royal family. There was thrill and sensuality in that thought. Imagine if you could wear the best of silks and eat the freshest of fruits, listen to the best musicians live in your court any time you please?

France had left me a taste of many things. Most of all, she taught me to not be afraid of expressing myself fearing that it would be too much. There is romance in expression, a quiet confidence that France urged me to recognise. France sure knew how to unlock that piece of my heart.

13

The Steam Engine Train Punctuates the Pause in Slyudyanka

The icy cold fresh morning air froze my cheeks, but my heart was smiling from the warmth of an idea. I was going to sit in a steam engine train and experience the classic Circum-Baikal vintage train called *Matanya* that runs along the world's largest lake, Baikal in Siberia. The anticipation had provided enough heat to warm my body in those sub-zero temperatures in late April, what some Siberians called a delightful start to summer.

I reached the Slyudyanka train station before noon and bought a ticket for the 1:30 p.m. train. I settled into the waiting room with over an hour to kill. Through the gaps in the frost-covered window, I spotted a church across the street from the one-room station. Walking towards it, I noticed that it was desperately in need of a paint job and some plastering on the side walls. But the bell tower looked impressive, so I decided to pay a visit.

I peeped inside the church but I didn't go in. Instead, I sat on the steps outside and wondered if I nursed too high expectations from the train journey. I had read plenty about the pre-Second World War Circum-Baikal train, which was a break away from the popular longest rail journey in the world, the Trans-Siberian railway. If my expectations were high, I was perhaps justified, I thought. I would find out soon enough.

My mind zipped back to the present, watching a bunch of boys play football and making a huge noise. I joined them and played for a few minutes only to be given a reality check of my physical stamina. Although the exercise warmed me up, my knees creaked, and my heart wanted to fling out of my chest. I had to sit back down to calm both my heart and enthusiasm.

With not much scope for people-watching in the tiny station, I prepared for a boring wait in the still almost-empty waiting room. Just then, a man wearing a red windbreaker sitting at an angle from me across the rows of seats shouted out loud, 'India!'

He gobbled up the last bit of his sandwich and then approached me. We shook hands and he introduced himself as Anton Krotov and the woman next to him as his wife, Katerina Boyarova.

Anton sported a scraggly beard and spoke animatedly in a strong Russian accent. His intense green eyes bore through my brown ones, leaving me feeling exposed, as though my exact thoughts were revealed through his study of my eyes. Anton spoke about his visit to the Satya Sai Baba ashram in Whitefield, Bangalore, almost a decade ago, making the connection to the city where I grew up.

'Is this your first time on this train?' I asked him.

'No no . . . I have done this circuit a few times. My mother has lived all her life in Russia and hadn't seen Lake Baikal. So, I brought her along on this train ride, which is the best way to experience the lake,' he said.

I shared my month-long Russia itinerary and we spoke in general about the pitfalls and the beauty of travelling in Russia, especially for foreigners. He excused himself to attend a phone call while Katerina and I continued to chat.

She leaned into me and whispered, 'You might not know but Anton is a celebrity world traveller. He is too modest to share it. But he has written many books and travelled the world all his life.'

At this point, Anton re-joined our conversation.

'Katerina tells me that you're a celebrity,' I said.

He laughed and looked at his wife. 'I wouldn't say celebrity. But yes, I've travelled quite a bit,' he said, still hesitant.

Katerina stepped in and shared more information, 'Not just quite a bit. Quite a lot, actually. Anton has travelled to over 110 countries and has written more than 50 books, all on travel, especially free travel. Some of his books are *Hitchhiking across India*, *Hitchhiking to Sudan*, *From -50 to +50*, covering travel in cold Siberia and warm Africa.'

I prodded him to share more information. He revealed that he founded the Academy of Free Travel in 1995 with the aim of promoting cross-cultural and cross-country information while encouraging travellers to explore possibilities for independent travel.

The academy organises hitchhiking expeditions and treks around the globe and Russia. 'Since 2007, we have been hosting Houses for Everyone. Anyone in any part of the world can open up a house—at their own cost—to travellers for free stay. The travellers must pitch in to do the housework and buy food to share with all. Everyone who stays as a guest shares resources and stories from around the globe. We have been running this successfully for many years now,' he explained.

'What is the motivation for the volunteers to open up their home to strangers?' I was curious.

Anton's eyes lit up as he shared his vision. 'It's the passion to promote travel, and to meet people from different world cultures. Imagine an Iraqi, Turk, Ethiopian, Chinese, and Chilean sitting at a table for dinner exchanging stories from their parts of the world. Besides, the volunteers open their homes only for a few months every year, not year-round. These dates and locations are announced on the website many months in advance so that travellers can plan accordingly.'

Anton was a ball of high energy, bouncing about with enthusiasm. He had been on this same train journey multiple times, but he expressed more excitement for it than I did.

He pulled out a large map of Lake Baikal and pointed to the route that we would be taking on the Circum-Baikal train. He spoke about every village and every landmark along the way.

'We will also be seeing Roerich's house. I'll show you,' he said, animatedly.

'Will the train be crowded? Do we need to rush to get a seat?' I asked.

'Not likely but let's go quickly and pick a good seat. Stay close to me,' he answered. His energy had infected me. Now, I was doubly excited for this steam engine train ride.

When the train was announced in Russian, he listened to the announcement with great attention and asked me to follow him quickly. There were only seven passengers waiting for this train, yet he made a dash for the platform asking his wife and mother to walk slowly while he blocked their seats. I felt there was no need to run but I followed him anyway and got into the two-bogie train, perhaps the shortest train I have ever sat in.

It looked like a toy train that carried the weight of history easy on its wheels. The seating plan inside the train was simple, with two-seater cushioned chairs lined up on either side.

We rushed into the empty bogie, and he blocked the seats right at the centre of the bogie while I took the next window seat and settled down. He called out for me and asked me to go outside with him so that we could click photos next to the engine before we set off.

As soon as the train started to move shortly after a high-pitched whistle, we were riding right next to Lake Baikal. If the window could be opened, I would be able to stretch out my hand right above the lake waters.

The train's movement, which was more enhanced when compared to the faster electric trains that are more popular today, reminded me of its uniqueness, the steam engine. This is one of the few steam engine trains operating in the world, was a tribute to a time in the past when transportation was revolutionised. The advent of the steam engine train was the exclamation point in the chapter of history that paved the way for industrialisation. The train I was now sitting in was a hat tip to that mega shift, a thank-you for showing us what coal, a boiler, and lots of hot water can do for our lives.

The cold and dark-grey afternoon stretched on with no respite for the rest of the day. It even snowed an hour into the train ride, which lent a magical other-worldly air to the stunning views of the lake on one side and mountains on the other.

I was lost in a land of dreams, fog, and clouds when I heard Anton constantly shuffling about. He could not sit still and went to the back of the train to look at the train track from the tiny open window. Curious, I followed him, and clicked photos of the burst of light just as the train exited the dark tunnels.

As I stood by the tiny circular window watching the train winding in and out of tunnels, so many metaphors came to mind. This train ride was so much like life itself, travelling through highs and lows, ups and downs, and changing sceneries at all times.

No matter where we are in our story today, it can expect to change; it *will* change. I saw the metaphor of the light at the end of the tunnel play out before me as the push-pull of the train chugged it slow and steady along the mountain path, taking us along on the ride of a lifetime.

The 89-km long Circum-Baikal railway line built in 1905 curves along the southern tip of the lake from Slyudyanka to Port Baikal and was part of the Trans-Siberian rail network before the Second World War.

The railway track itself is an engineering marvel with 424 engineering constructions along the way, making way for 39 tunnels cutting through mountains on the journey. Also, 14 km of supporting walls had to be built along the line.

The rail route is now used more as a tourist attraction with tourist trains running to full house, complete with snacks and activities along the five-hour journey during peak summer season. Adventure-seekers even get off the train and camp for a few days at picturesque spots by the lake.

The train stops at several villages along the way, which makes it an attractive and cheap mode of transportation for the locals. On my train ride, several villagers entered and left the train carrying farm equipment, large bags of supplies as well as groceries. This was a perfect window-seat view of Siberian village life.

The train moved at a slow pace, stopping often. Every train station was a thatched-roof single-room wooden structure against the backdrop of the lake and mountains. I saw that the stops had a kilometre number mentioned but no name. I asked Anton about this, and he was ever so glad to explain the logic.

'The Circum-Baikal train is thought about in terms of kilometre. Every kilometre along the way holds a lot of importance considering the amount of engineering work that has gone into laying this railway track. The amount of earth moved to build just one km of this railway line could fill up 400 carriages!' he said, pausing to allow me time to process the magnitude of those numbers.

He continued, 'Since the days of the construction, each kilometre was referred to by the number along the line. The stop names also stuck according to the kilometre number.'

'But this track is 89-km long. How is it that some stations are at 102 km and 139 km?'

'Ah! Good question. When the Circum-Baikal railway was connected to the Trans-Siberian line, the kilometres along the Circum-Baikal track were measured from the Irkutsk exchange station. Port Baikal was 72 km from Irkutsk station and the other end of Slyudyanka was at 161 km. So, the names of the stations are between 72 and 161 km. And those numbers stuck even after the Circum-Baikal line started running independent of the Trans-Siberian.'

Anton added that I made a good decision to take the local train rather than the tourist version, which sometimes runs on a steam locomotive with retro-style cars designed to impress tourists.

'It is a lot of show and noise for the same experience. In fact, this is more authentic. You can see the quiet village life in a journey like this one.'

We clicked more photos of tunnels through the faded glass window that was heavily scratched and stained. We got off the train at every station and snapped more photos. I was glad to have the company of someone so enthusiastic that I could express my enthusiasm with him without seeming foolish.

Anton didn't care about how he appeared to the world around him. He simply was himself at all times. He took in his environment in its entirety, even if it meant he looked odd craning his neck or widening his eyes in surprise or letting out a low hum to approve of how the sandwich tasted. He was right here, present at all times, for every moment.

It was the most spiritual quality. It is also difficult to retain the here-and-now presence while on the road because the road invites the mind to unravel parts of the past and to imagine the future.

At one station, Anton disappeared, I couldn't see him anywhere. Katerina was still standing by the window, so I asked her.

'Anton requested the engine driver if he and his mother could ride with the driver for a short stretch. Till the next station, they are with the driver,' she said.

When they returned at the next stop, I asked Anton about the experience. He was ecstatic and showed me photos of piles of coal and the engine driver's seat. His mother, though, was expressionless throughout.

I spent some time sitting by myself looking out the window at the breathtaking landscapes. The train was moving unbelievably close to the water and at some spots, the gentle waves of the lake kissed the train tracks. I saw lush green grass, the calm lake with dancing ripples, a light snowfall, and imposing mountains as the train sliced between the water on one side and mountains on the other, going in and out of tunnels, metaphoric of life's never-ending journey of winding roads, highs and lows.

Anton called out to me just as I was getting into a deep state of meditative rumination. 'This was Roerich's house, which is now a museum. Well, it is one of his many homes.

You know him right, the famous painter?' he said. I nodded, telling Anton about Roerich's connection to Bangalore. Svetoslav Roerich married Indian actress Devika Rani and the couple lived till their last years in an estate on the outskirts of Bangalore.

It was a marvellous experience to see Roerich's quaint family home from the tiny train window. An entire page of history opened up through this sight, making me marvel, yet again, at travel's power to take us back in time and into the future with ease.

Anton stared at the home for a few minutes and then started to tell me about the tourist areas along this train journey that are still in operation. These tourist places are themed according to the forest reserves maintained by the government. One is the Taiga theme at 134 km on this train line, and another is the Coniferous theme at 98 km.

By the time the train stopped at Port Baikal, the last ferry out had already left. Anton said that he and his family carried sleeping bags and would find a place to spend the night. The place was barren with only the train station building and nothing else around it.

I walked to the river bed and managed to team up with a couple of backpackers and hire a boat to cross the river. I bid goodbye to Anton, Katerina, and his mother hoping to see them again somewhere sometime.

The boat ride was thrilling and dangerously fast in sharp contrast to the languorous pace of the train journey. The cold air hit me with such force that my face and any exposed skin instantly went numb.

Yet, this was such an adventure that the couple from Slovakia and I managed to hold our phones up on the bouncing boat to click photos of the river and our boat ride. In the course of our conversation, we learnt that we were booked in hotels along the same road. We shared the four-kilometre taxi ride into Listvyanka, where I settled into my cosy room and turned up the heater on full power.

I was the only guest in the entire resort-style hotel and enjoyed the quiet time with the forest behind me and the lake within a few meters. I was truly in the lap of nature and let its beauty wash over me. This was one of my most romantic travel experiences yet. It had all the ingredients of a classic Victorian-era journey: A steam engine train, slow pace, a gentle lake, imposing mountains, intermittent snowfall, enthusiastic company to open up my mind, a trip down memory lane, and the room to let the future show me bits of herself.

As if on cue, it started snowing again, the quiet forest submitting to the fall of tiny white specks. The forest stood strong and steady while being soft enough to surrender. She was teaching me the power of being present.

That day, so many experiences were showing me this same power of presence, be it Anton or the train or the forest around me. To be fully present demands great spiritual maturity. I have failed more times than I have succeeded in practising the power of now. But every time I succeeded, I grew stronger. I felt a spiritual muscle, a muscle of willpower, the muscle of focus being flexed. It was also telling me that to keep trying is all that matters.

It snowed all night, and I woke up to the play of sun and snow in the Siberian summer. It was another day. Time for another adventure.

I BELIEVE

This is faith reloaded. These are places that brought me back to my centre, reminding me of the unwavering faith that sits deep within the layers of countless tugs and shoves of the demanding tech-fuelled life. These are places that stand as inner temples of consciousness that no storm can sway out of shape.

14

Forging a Divine Connection at the Dwarkadhish Temple

The drumbeats echoed and reverberated in the narrow hallway creating an aura of grandness. Something important was about to happen. The insistent thumping of the drums were a call to draw your attention and to not miss this most crucial event unfolding before your eyes.

The loud and steady drumming drowned out every other sound, both internal and external. I had always believed that silence was the best way to go inward. Here, as I stood in line to see the famous Krishna idol at the Dwarkadhish temple in Dwarka at the western tip of India, I experienced, for the first time, the power of sound in pulling me inward.

The beats commanded my mind to be present in the here and now. The echoes tugged at my heart, pulling me into the depths of the whirlpool of divinity. I was in an echo chamber where all I could see, hear, and feel was Krishna. I stayed put in the hall with all my heart and soul. The sound was a powerful, metrical boom.

When I closed my eyes, I could see a pure white cloud laid out like a carpet in the blue sky. The white carpet was an invitation to visit the lord of love, Krishna. I was walking on that white carpet.

The drumbeats brought my attention to the cold stone floor under my feet. Between the ornate pillars, I caught a glimpse of light filtering in through the blue sky. Pigeons flew about as though in merriment. I inhaled the comforting scent of camphor. It is the assuring incense, which tells me that I am safe in the arms of the earth. It tells me that I am exactly where I am supposed to be.

I inched forward in the crowd, being sucked into its magnetic pull towards the sanctum sanctorum. I saw a sea of faces around me: Closed eyes, chanting lips, and devout surrender. Some hands were folded while some were cupped in gentle beseeching.

The woman next to me let the rhythm seep into every pore of her being. Her hips moved to the beats and her heart sang a sweet melody that only she could hear. Eyes closed and face smiling in ecstatic bliss; she was celebrating the Krishna in her.

The sights, sounds and smells beckoned me to find my personal moment. I didn't have to try too hard because in only a few seconds, I felt a powerful surge of pure love in my heart. It was a magical experience unlike any other. The intellectual in me was too weak for the emotion that flooded my being. At once, I was water, I was air, I was the earth, and I was the fire carrying life. I was all of it in this singular moment. Is this what they call divine bliss? A tear of knowing escaped my eye.

My spirit and being were ecstatic in the moment but my mind wanted in on the action. What is this feeling? What is this moment of nothingness that holds everything? My mind wanted to articulate it. But the tug of elation was so powerful that I was swayed by it. I inched closer towards the sanctum sanctorum, and then amid the sea of bobbing heads, I got the first glimpse of Krishna.

My heart leapt in joy. From the core of my spirit, I felt waves of peace pulsating all through my body. The mind stood no chance of overtaking this powerful spiritual experience. I was in a trance. The music only took me to a higher state of joy with every passing moment.

The next few minutes went by too quickly. In only a few seconds, I had a full view of the Krishna idol. The main deity was dressed in a bright yellow silk kurta with a fuchsia pink border. It had pearls and colourful shiny beads embroidered on it. He also wore an off-white dhoti. A peacock feather was fixed to his pink head covering, also heavily decorated in beads and golden lace.

Krishna sat on a swing. One priest danced to the beats while holding an elaborate pyramid-shaped lamp holder made of brass. Wicks dipped in ghee were lit up and arranged along the steps of the lamp holder, making it a tiny mountain of flames. The dancing priest waved the pyramid of lights towards Krishna and sang and swayed to the ecstasy.

A second priest held one end of a rope tied to the swing and gently rocked the swing back and forth, visibly lost in the moment. I got to stand before the idol and look straight into Krishna's eyes for only a couple of seconds before I had to move out of the queue and make way for the throng of waiting devotees.

I stepped out of the line and into the cool December air still giddy from the experience from a few moments ago. My heart was pounding and my arms were shaking from the waves of high energy coursing through my body. I did not know how to identify what I felt at the moment because it was unlike anything I had ever experienced.

I walked out to the temple courtyard, where other smaller temples with stone sculptures on their walls stood meters apart. I sat out in the open on the floor leaning against a structure with floral stone carvings. Facing the main sanctum sanctorum, I tried to make sense of what Krishna meant to me.

Lord Krishna was a familiar mythological figure to me as are the many deities that belong to the colourfully rich plethora of Hindu mythology. Most famous of all is Krishna's narration of the Bhagavad Gita to Arjuna on the battlefield of Kurukshetra, which features in the epic Mahabharata. But did I really know Krishna? I did not.

I was amused by Krishna's antics. I chuckled at his flirtatious manner and his way of looking at life in a lighter vein. I was in awe of his ability to remain stress-free in the most difficult situations. I understood that Krishna embodied life's biggest secret of how to live in the moment. I knew Krishna from my mind, but I hadn't connected with him in my heart. This connection was plugged in today in a most non-fussed manner.

Sure, I travelled all the way to Dwarka for an experience. In that sense, I went out seeking him. But I did not realise that Krishna would come alive in me in such a boldly vivid manner. I could feel Krishna in my pulse, sending out joyful energy all around me.

For this to happen, my mind had to take a pause. I could not intellectualise everything. I had to surrender to the moment. This was the first time that my body had taken charge and surrendered without my preparing for it in advance or willing it. My only preparation was to walk up the fifty-six steps, known as the *Swarga Dwar* (Door to Heaven) leading to the sanctum sanctorum. There was feverish anticipation that I would witness a beautifully decorated Krishna idol. But I did not expect the deep impact this visit would have on my body.

This moment made me understand surrender. The peaceful energy radiating from the sanctum sanctorum had shut down the persistent thoughts that kept my mind hostage. Don't think. *Feel*, the moment was saying.

I sat in silence for a long time, simply allowing the energy to stay in me for as long as possible. I did not check the time; I did not push to get up and leave. I did not feel or want anything else but to be in that moment.

Krishna had introduced me to that vast sea of consciousness, and just a dip of my being in that sea had coloured me a bright white of peace. This was possible because, deep down, I believed. I had faith in the presence of something big and beautiful. Belief is half the journey travelled.

In my short trip to various parts of Gujarat in western India, I saw faith in many forms. In Ahmedabad, I saw believers praying just after sunrise at the Sidi Sayyed Mosque. This mosque has been home to devout followers of Islam since 1573.

I was at the Somnath temple, the gorgeous seashore temple, where chants of Om Namah Shivaya filled the salty air. Devotees stood for hours in long lines to get close to the Shiva energy that they believed will keep them company in peace and good health for a long time.

I went to the 400-year-old Dattatreya Temple in Kalo Dungar or the Black Hills in the Kutch region of Gujarat. Tourists flock to this remote region to see the India Bridge beyond which is our neighbouring country Pakistan.

Legend has it that when Lord Dattatreya was wandering these hills, he encountered a bunch of hungry jackals. The Lord let the hungry jackals eat him but every time the jackals took a bite of his body, it would regenerate itself. Visitors believe that it is good luck to visit this temple at the Black Hills on the way to the White Desert, India's expansive salt marsh called Rann of Kutch. It is such intense belief that drives us.

On the way up the Black Hills, my car driver, Rohan Gor, stopped at a point called Magnetic Hill. At this point, it is believed that any metal is pulled in the reverse direction by an invisible force. Scientists conducted experiments to test the soil and rocks in the vicinity and did not find any scientific evidence for this inexplicable freak of nature.

Rohan stopped the car with the gear in neutral and took his feet off the pedals. The car was pulled in the reverse direction uphill at a speed of about ten kilometres per hour. My sceptical mind couldn't believe that this could be simply magic. Yet, there was no explanation. I did not believe, so I did not really have fun. I looked around at the tourists around me who were clicking videos and photos of this 'miracle'. They certainly seemed to be having more fun than the sceptical me.

Belief is a natural state of being while suspicion leads to stress. A believer, of religion at least, truly believes that nothing is an accident. She believes that everything is mandated by a higher force, a God, a divine energy. Belief has a greater role to play in our lives when we find that certain obvious things have no meaning but certain covert things carry a lot of meaning. It may be invisible. It may be difficult or impossible to find empirical evidence for these things, yet they make so much sense to us. They might be giving us purpose and meaning beyond our comprehension and ability to explain how or why.

I went to the Gopi Talav outside Dwarka. A short walk from the main highway, I saw small temples and rows of streetside shops selling Gopi Chandan, the curative clay that is found only on the banks of this lake.

The story goes that when Krishna moved to Dwarka from Vrindavan, the *gopis* could not bear to be separated from him. So, they came to Dwarka to meet Krishna. On a glorious full moon night, they performed *Raas Leela*, the dance of divine love, in a lake that came to be known as

Gopi Talav. Not wanting to leave Dwarka, the gopis merged with the lake and turned to clay on its banks. This special clay is known to have healing properties and cures skin disorders. To this day, believers throng this lakebed to carry back blocks of dried clay in the hope that it heals and protects them.

This is the power of belief.

I rode to another temple along this highway outside Dwarka. It was the Rukmini Temple, which has a myth of its own. The temple is dedicated to Rukmini, Krishna's wife and queen. The specialty of this 2,500-year-old temple is that water is offered to the deity here. Water is not just offered but also taken as an offering from the Goddess. It is believed that if you drink the holy water from this temple, you will never be thirsty or want for water in life.

The mythological story behind it is that Krishna invited sage Durvasa to visit him in Dwarka. The sage agreed but on the condition that Krishna and Rukmini escort him to Dwarka by pulling his chariot. When they were on the outskirts of Dwarka, a thirsty Rukmini asked Krishna for water. Krishna prodded the earth using just his toe and water from the Ganga River sprouted from the ground. Rukmini had her fill of water but forgot to ask Sage Durvasa if he would like some. The sage felt slighted by this neglect and cursed Rukmini that she would be fated to live apart from Krishna all the time.

The Rukmini Devi Temple is said to be the place where Krishna drew water from the ground. I, too, stood in line to drink a glass of water offered by the priest.

I then rode back to Dwarka, wanting to be near the Dwarkadhish Temple. I sat on the narrow alleys of Dwarka about fifty meters away from the base of the fifty-six steps leading to the temple. A young man looked towards me with interest. As I sat watching the world go by, he was observing me sitting on the banks of the river.

Finally, the twenty-one-year-old Jayaraj Jadeja, who ran a travel agency on the banks of the Gomti River, walked towards me and struck up a conversation. In his initial introduction, he made it a point to mention that he belonged to the Jadeja clan of royalty in Gujarat. He asked me if I would like an aerial view of the old streets of Dwarka and the river. I nodded. So, he led me to the terrace of his shop. From here I witnessed a mass of people climbing the fifty-six steps for their experience of Krishna.

On the other side, we both stood and watched a unique ritual. This was the ritual of draping a saree to the Gomti River, giving her a gift, and asking for protection and prosperity in exchange. Now, how would one go about draping a saree to the river?

A temple dedicated to Goddess Gomti stood on the banks of the river. In the ritual led by a family of devotees, the head priest tied one end of a specially designed saree to the finger of Goddess Gomti. In the midst of much fanfare, music, drumbeats, and dancing, the other end of the saree, which was rolled in a huge bundle, was unfurled over the flowing river. To cross the river, the devotees used three boats with many arms holding up the edges of the saree. It was not one but about 15 sarees stitched together end-to-end to make a long piece of fabric. From my vantage point on the terrace, it looked like a half-a-kilometre long, colourful runway.

I asked Jayaraj what he thought of this ritual.

'It is all about faith,' he said, his eyes not leaving the people or the saree on the river. 'If you believe it is, it is. If you don't believe, it isn't.'

I asked him what he believed. He smiled but did not respond.

The next morning, I wished to visit the Dwarkadhish temple again. I saw Jayaraj sitting at his shop and asked him if he would like to join me. Without taking his eyes off his computer, he said that he was currently in the middle of a fight with Krishna.

I asked him what he meant. 'I had asked Him for something and He still hasn't given it to me. Till He fulfils my wish I will not see Him. I am angry with Him.'

'So, you have deep faith in Him after all. It is more than you will admit,' I said.

'I am not separate from Him. He is not separate from me. We are one. But we still argue and fight like friends,' he said.

What Jayaraj expressed was beyond the question of belief. He was living the divine experience in his daily life and had travelled much further than the initial dilemma of 'to be' or 'not to be'. He just was. He was completely immersed in the Krishna energy and saw no separation of this energy from any other part of his life.

Ultimately, that is where we desire faith to take us—a place of no doubt and unquestioning surrender.

15

The Monks Who Laughed When the Bumblebee Stung Me in Phnom Penh

Is it spiritual to laugh at another's pain? The monks at Wat Botum monastery in Phnom Penh, Cambodia, didn't care even if it wasn't. A bee stung me at the monastery grounds when I was standing with the monks. I screamed my lungs out in pain, and the monks laughed their hearts out. I then laughed with them. Suddenly, the pain was gone. Let me rewind to the beginning of this story.

Travel is an indulgent birthday gift that I give myself every year. My birthday comes two days after New Year's Day, so all I do is stretch the year-end holiday to include my birthday and a little beyond.

Since I started solo travel in my mid-twenties, I have been able to keep up this ritual birthday gift of travel experiences almost every year. Wherever I am in the world, I also tend to follow the birthday ritual of visiting a sacred place. I'm not fussed about it being a temple or church or monastery. It doesn't even need to be a consecrated place. I am perfectly fine sending my birthday wishes to the universe through the beach, the mountains, the tall trees, or the chirping birds.

I was in Phnom Penh, Cambodia, on one such birthday-holiday. I had travelled across Cambodia for two weeks and was on my last stop at Phnom Penh before flying back home the day after my birthday. It was unusual for me to fuss over clothes, but on that trip, I was prepared with a brand-new dress that I had carried to wear on the special day. So, I wore the dress in my favourite teal colour and set out to find a quiet Buddhist monastery where I could sit in stillness for a while.

I called a bike-taxi and asked the rider to drop me at a quiet and peaceful monastery. He rode to the heart of Phnom Penh, informing me that he would be dropping me off at a monastery called Wat Botum (pronounced What Bottom. I'm kidding. I didn't catch how exactly it is pronounced).

The rider slowed down when he saw barricades preventing any vehicles from going further along that road. He stopped by the side of the street and pointed towards a tiny gate indicating that it was the entrance. I figured that this was a side entrance and so I went in. The monastery was quiet, not a sound coming from any of the small, square rooms built across the grounds. Many fruit trees sprung up, breaking through the concrete floor. Cement benches were constructed around tree trunks to form seating areas.

Tiny buildings dotted the monastery land. Maroon robes hung from the clotheslines and swayed only slightly in the gentle breeze that kept alive the morning's cool. I walked along and didn't see anyone for almost ten full minutes. Then I saw two monks walking towards me. They looked at me strangely, as though surprised by my presence here, but smiled and walked on. It was then that I wondered if I was wandering through a restricted area.

I went on and saw a door opening out to a hall. A golden Buddha idol sat on an elevated platform at one end of the hall. It looked like a smaller meditation space attached to the larger temple.

I walked in and was greeted by a man who spoke English. He wasn't wearing the Buddhist robes and seemed to be working in the office attached to the temple.

'How can I help you?' he asked with the gentlest smile that can take the tense edge off a bad day, if you were having one.

His congenial approach triggered honesty from me, 'Today is my birthday and I wanted to sit in some corner of the monastery and meditate if that's okay?' Revealing to a stranger that it was my birthday came out awkwardly and suddenly. That's unlike me, I chuckled to myself. He smiled and asked me to wait.

I looked around the mostly empty hall in which even the gentlest of steps echoed through the room. Five minutes later, the man was leading an old monk towards me. Frail with wrinkled skin that had collected age and wisdom over the decades, the monk had bright eyes that sparkled with youth, enthusiasm, and a glint of mischief. His maroon robe was oversized, perhaps it looked that way because of the loose manner in which he draped it across his right shoulder.

The office manager asked the monk to wait and rushed to get a chair for him. It was a low seat like a throne with elaborate silver carving on the backrest. A cushion was laid on it and the manager helped the monk lower himself into the seat.

Then the manager disappeared for a few more minutes. He brought a tiny table and set a few things on it, including a large bowl of water, a smaller empty bowl, a white sticky paste in a cup, bands of thick cotton thread, a carved silver wand, and a bowl filled with beads and other trinkets.

The man then spoke to the monk close to his ear, presumably explaining that it was my birthday. The monk looked at me and smiled like an old knowing soul would smile at a beginner on the journey. He gestured for me to sit down. I sat cross-legged before him the way one sits before a guru. The monk closed his eyes and meditated for a few minutes. Then he started chanting some mantras.

The hall reverberated with the chants, the lilting tone of the monk's voice filling my senses. The energy in the hall felt sacred, and I sat in reverence for this experience. The manager who had left the hall returned by the time the chanting stopped. He then helped the monk with the rituals. The monk held his hands over the empty bowl on the table while the manager poured water to wash the monk's hands, allowing it to collect in the bowl.

The monk sprinkled water on his head and all around him. The manager asked me to sit by the monk's feet. I did, and the monk held the bowl of water in his hands, closed his eyes and chanted for a long time. With eyes remaining closed, he gently poured the water over my head.

The cold water trickled down my skin, sending shivers of chill up my spine. It was a rude wake-up jolt. My hair and clothes were dripping wet. The monk then pointed to my right hand, and I held it out. He tied a blue band around my wrist, continuing to chant mantras. He scooped out a generous amount of the sticky white glue-like paste and smeared it all over the band around my wrist.

We sat in companionable silence for a few minutes, communing with the invisible forces in that hall and beyond. A potent force was palpable to me in those rituals. It felt like a benevolent, wise energy watching over us and smiling. The monk said something in Cambodian. The manager told me that he wished me luck, safe travels, and happiness all my life. My eyes welled up on hearing such a pure intent from a stranger.

I came here not knowing exactly what I would find. I sought peace of mind. I sought a place where I wanted to safely allow my intentions to be known so that I could set goals and make this a time of reflection and motivation.

In my quest for a quiet space, I was given so much more. I was given the gift of a well-wisher's pure intentions for me. It is said that such prayers—which carry no selfish motive—work best as the universe is listening and recording everything. I don't know about this, but I believe that everything happens for a reason. Meeting this wise old monk felt like an encounter designed by the universe, the ultimate aim of which I may never know.

All I knew was that I felt peaceful being here. I felt heard and understood even though this was the first time I was meeting this monk. Carrying the belief that everything is connected and there is a purpose to every meeting and every situation, even when we may not know what it is, is a deep level of trust with the universe that can lead to greater degrees of peace.

Developing this trust for the universe is difficult as it requires wading in large swathes of the unknown with only your own desire to lead you further along. Entering the monastery and being open to a spiritual experience was rooted in my personal brand of belief. I didn't know it then, but I know it now: To believe takes courage.

It took courage to walk into the monastery seeking something not knowing what it is. It also took courage to wander in an unknown place. It took courage to be open to a new experience with the monk. When I was open in this manner, I was gifted with the monk's blessings and prayers.

I smiled and thanked him. I then asked if I could click a picture with the monk. He readily agreed and stood up with support from the manager. He asked the manager to straighten his robes so that he looked good in the picture while I pulled the camera out of my bag.

Still dripping wet, I clicked a photo of his smiling face. Then the manager clicked a shot of the monk and me. The monk turned to leave, and I quickly asked the manager what kind of offering I need to make. He was taken aback but gave me his gentle smile again and said, 'Nothing at all.' I accepted it.

Travel had taught me enough to know that not everything is transactional. But my trained business mind needed to be sure. I chatted with the manager some more and asked if I was allowed to explore the monastery. He said I was free to walk anywhere.

I thanked him profusely and left the hall with an open heart and a deep sense of gratitude for all my experiences, good and bad. I walked around the monastery with my camera slung around my neck. I still didn't see too many monks walking about. This must be their prayer time or rest time, I thought.

I passed by a room with over twenty monks seated on the floor around a long, low table. They were having a meal. I smiled at them and they smiled back. I approached them slowly and sat on the steps leading into the room. The table was filled with plates of all kinds of food.

I saw cut fruits, steamed vegetables, and other foods that I did not recognise.

'May I chat with you?' I asked. They giggled. I wasn't sure they spoke English. I asked for permission to click photos by lifting my camera up in their direction. The monk who sat near the door, closest to me, nodded. So, I started to click their photos. They kept looking at me with curiosity and the shyness is a typical trait of rural dwellers that don't often see people from other cultures.

I tried to ask a few questions but they didn't answer. Nobody there seemed to speak English. I continued to sit among them for a long time as they ate and looked at me.

Just then a bee started buzzing about me. It was an aggressive sneaky rascal that was loud, quick, and on offense mode. I tried to shoo it away with my hands, but the bee only got more aggressive. I shrieked when it tried to hit at my eyes.

The monks found this exchange between the bee and me fascinating. They laughed slowly at first. When the bee just wouldn't let go, I started to flail my hands wildly hoping that the bee would find another place to go. I must have made for quite a comical picture because the monks laughed even louder this time.

The war between me and the bee intensified. I moved my right arm in a giant sweep to push it away. That's when it showed me who is boss. It stung my arm. I screamed more out of panic than pain. The monks laughed out loud as though a comedy film was playing out before them. I inspected the red bite mark and decided to get first aid although it wasn't looking severe at all.

The monks were still laughing at my unexpected adventure. I looked around the room and saw that they weren't laughing at me. They were laughing at the situational comedy. They were being present in the here and now. They found something funny, so, they laughed. Their innocence travelled to their eyes. At that moment, something in my heart opened wide. I laughed with them, and we were all now laughing together. And I had the bee to thank for this moment.

A monk walked into the room from an inner room and said something. It sounded like an instruction. The monks immediately stood up and ritualistically walked around the table clockwise. They now looked serious and walked with purpose and intent with eyes on the floor. The smiles and laughter had faded. It was my cue to leave.

I walked towards the main temple. I saw barricades again, the same kind that had prevented the bike taxi from dropping me at the main gate. I walked around the barricades and arrived at an opening where a grand banquet was in session.

A large tent in white silk provided sunshade to about a dozen round tables, also decked up in white silk. It looked like an armed forces reception as most guests were formally dressed in army, air force, and navy uniforms. The women were in their best silk gowns. A lavish buffet spread was organised for them at the landing of the steps just outside the main pagoda.

I walked around this gathering and went up the short flight of stairs to enter the main pagoda. I could see the golden Buddha sitting in all his majesty and power of simplicity. I walked a few steps into the large hall towards the Buddha. I turned to the opposite side of the hall and stopped in my tracks when I saw a group of men staring at me.

I could feel all their pairs of eyes on me. From the few seconds that I stood there, my mind registered rich velvet cloth, gold embroidery, royal silk robes, a grand buffet—a spread of exotic foods laid out on a low table—and shocked faces that a backpacker had coolly walked into their private gathering.

A young woman in a *sampot*, the Cambodian national dress, ran towards me. She ran as fast as her tight wraparound-like dress would allow. 'May I help you?' she asked me in the most coherent English accent that I had heard in my fifteen days in Cambodia. If she were tense or anxious about my presence in the hall, she did a perfect job of masking it with her practiced composure.

I was struck by her beauty. Her large eyes searched mine enquiringly. Her flawlessly smooth skin was either the work of expert make-up or inheritance, or hard work. It took me a moment to recover from her beauty and the white light bouncing off her glistening lipstick.

'I'm here to visit the temple,' I said, vaguely pointing towards the Buddha idol, unconvinced myself, still struck by her beauty.

'The temple is closed for a private gathering today. You'll have to come later,' she said, in a matter-of-fact, rehearsed manner. She then touched the small of my back gently leading me outside.

I did turn to get one quick glance at the grandly dressed young man, clearly the main guest of the event, wearing a crown made of gold with velvety silk dressing. Around him sat a coterie of men, all still staring at me. I couldn't tell if they were shocked or confused. I don't even know if my gatecrashing would jeopardise someone's job.

As soon as I walked out, a security guard in plain-clothes came rushing towards me to usher me out all the way outside the gate before firmly locking it in place. He would probably get a yelling.

The woman's beauty stayed with me for a long time. I have not forgotten her face. I never will. I walked around the rest of the temple grounds, clicking photos of the elaborate pagoda design and a few sculptures of mythological figures that received a grand display on the monastery's walls.

I saw a monk relaxing on a bench. I asked him about the banquet by the main temple. I could gather from his broken English that the Cambodian prince was hosting this lunch for the armed forces. I didn't understand the occasion for the party.

I tried to find out how it was that they were allowed to dine inside the main pagoda hall. He couldn't understand my question. So, I gave up. I was nevertheless thrilled that I had somewhat gatecrashed the Cambodian prince's party.

I walked out of the monastery and along the Tonle Sap River towards the famous FCC restaurant, Foreign Correspondents' Club. The second floor of this restaurant offered stunning views of the river and the modest Phnom Penh skyline. Sipping on chilled beer and biting into wafers, I smiled to myself thinking about the delightfully unique experience this birthday offered.

Blessed by an eighty-year-old Buddhist monk, bit by a bee, laughed at by monks, and gatecrashed the Cambodian prince's party—all on the same day. Now *that* is difficult to beat.

16

Seeking Bargains and Buddhism in the Business District of Tsim Sha Tsui

Hong Kong is packed with people. The one pigeonhole image that comes to mind when I think of Hong Kong is tall square buildings with square windows, square AC units protruding from walls, clothes hanging to dry on the grills outside the windows, and pigeons flying near there.

I found this stereotype to match perfectly on my ride from the airport to the Tsim Sha Tsui neighbourhood. The buildings are compressed, packed to fit maximum people in minimum space. But I also saw water, greenery, mountains, and rich natural resources hold their own in this financial capital where greed and ambition dictate the landscape and energy.

I was in Hong Kong for only a day each on my way to and back from Canada. In my few hours here, I did not expect to find much else to experience other than the typical images of commerce and a fast pace of life that accommodates ambitious financial goals. But Hong Kong surprised me.

Tucked away in this city of a-surprise-a-turn were little places of calm and culture that obstinately held on against waves of sweeping urbanism. My travel here was all about stumbling upon these surprises.

Hong Kong has too many people. The population density of Hong Kong as of 2023 was over 6,750 persons per sq. km.

Hotel rooms in Tsim Sha Tsui, the glitzy, neon-lit nightlife centre, reflected this space crunch. It was not until I visited Hong Kong that I understood the value of large-sized hotel rooms. They give you the space to breathe and to claim your presence in a city, even if for a short while.

My room in a mid-budget hotel barely fit my bag and me. Standing at the centre of the room I couldn't stretch my arms out wide. I had to jump over my bag to get to the window. The single bed, the size of a railway berth, covered more than half the room. The bathroom was a tiny cubicle with a frosted glass sliding door. I could touch the door from where I slept on the bed. It was the smallest hotel room that I had ever stayed in.

I wanted to peep out the sixth-floor window, so I opened the awning window. A pigeon flew uncomfortably close to me. Also, there wasn't much of a view. I only saw a street and a tree. So, I tried with all my might to close the window and it wouldn't shut.

I called the reception for help, and they sent a man to fix it. I had to wait outside the room so that he could go in and shut the window as two people couldn't stand in the room at the same time.

I wasn't going to be cooped up in this small room. So, I stepped out with a plan to return only when I was ready to sleep. Walking past the crowded streets, it seemed like everyone else had made a similar plan.

I set out to experience both the calm and chaos of Hong Kong. I allowed the city to lead me. I believed that there are oases of calm in this buzzing city, but I wasn't going to look up a city guide to tell me where I could find it. I was going to walk around and see if I could stumble upon something that stirred my soul.

The rushed manner of queuing up in Hong Kong did not surprise me. I noticed in the buses and metros the typical

South-East Asian style of rushing toward the door with scant attention to who else is around or who might be in the way.

I tend to hang back when people start to fall over me. I have missed buses and trains because of my tendency to want physical distance from strangers. I stood in line to ride the Peak Tram up to the famed Victoria Peak.

On this tourist-friendly tram ride, I was at the start of the line but when the tram arrived, those standing behind me in line had magically got into the tram before me and claimed all the window seats. I made it to the last available seat when I got in. I still don't know how to explain what happened. This was magical chaos.

I wondered if the famed view of the city lights from the vantage point at the peak would inspire calm in me. I was about to find out.

The tram ride was everything I had heard friends say it would be—steep and spectacular with changing views of the Hong Kong skyline. I spent time looking at an urban mass of buildings from Victoria Peak. This place had the highest number of skyscrapers in the world, which was double that of its nearest rival, New York.

This was, no doubt, a great tribute to architecture and human engineering. I marvelled at the talent and the intense planning that would have gone into creating this universe of cement blocks and bright lights. But my soul wasn't stirred. My eyes were taking in beautiful scenery but I felt an almost flat nothingness. What is it about Hong Kong that makes people go back to it? I wanted to peek inside this city's heart.

I rode the bus back downhill and sat by the waterfront watching the sun set and the moon rise over Hong Kong's buildings. On this full moon night, the moonshine reflecting on the water was absorbed in the shimmer of the building neon signs that were too bright and glitzy. The water looked like silver liquid dancing in a large container.

These reflections on the water triggered a metaphoric reflection of my inner self. I sat for a long time watching the ripples ebb and rise, mirroring my own state of mind on most days. The neon signs and the millions of tiny dots from the city lights bouncing off the water's surface seemed to put the water under the spotlight. The water seemed uncomfortable with this excessive attention, yet it had no choice but to continue being.

I walked to the Temple Street Night Market in Jordon, a few blocks from the Tsim Sha Tsui promenade. Several fancy cars and convertibles grazed the roads. I particularly looked for Rolls-Royces but spotted only two. It was strange, considering that Hong Kong has more Rolls Royces per person than any other city in the world.

Buzzing with life and bargains, the night market had for sale cheap electronics that you didn't know you needed. Drones, music speakers, phone accessories, wires, fancy LED alarm clocks, vintage-looking radio sets, the list is endless.

The market was busy, alive, and colourful. I heard at this global street market various foreign accents of world travellers and shoppers. It smelt like a mix of smoke, meats, and an assortment of scents wafting from the nearby Dai Pai Dongs, roadside food and noodles stalls.

The scents did not inspire any memories, nor did they repel my senses in any way. These were unfamiliar smells. And I felt nothing for them.

I walked through the market twice, end to end, and noticed that you would always find the same item cheaper at another store if you kept looking. Although shopping at the street markets of Hong Kong is about mastering the art of bargaining, a lot of it has to do with knowing when to stop when you really want an item. It's a tricky game, especially if you don't know the worth of an item and have to just make a wild guess.

In such situations, the shopkeepers were not too eager to sell. They bargained only up to a point and then asked you to get out if they decided that they didn't want to sell to you.

I watched a few such transactions from a distance but could not understand how these exchanges worked. I felt stressed to continue being in a place that was unpredictable and centred entirely on a give and take. It felt like an impersonal zone, and I left immediately.

The assault on the senses at the market tired me out, and I needed some quiet. This was too urban, too much of a city. So, I returned to my tiny hotel room and lay on the bed. Will I find any place of stability and calm at all here in the few hours of my stay? I decided to find out the next day.

When I woke up, I decided to visit the famous Man Mo Temple. After getting off the subway, I walked along the quiet, tree-lined streets in a residential neighbourhood. Away from the buzz of Nathan Road's shopping streets and malls, this place was slower with nobody in a rush to get anywhere or do anything.

I reached the temple and was taken aback by my first glimpse. It was hard to believe that Man Mo Temple, which is rated as one of the must-see places in Hong Kong, could be so small and unimpressive from the outside.

The temple stood against the backdrop of tall buildings with square windows, AC units, and clothes hanging out to dry. Warily, I stepped into the temple compound, not knowing what to expect. A wave of calm immediately enveloped me. I let out a sigh of relief. I felt as though the temple was inviting me in to be myself and it would not demand anything from me in return.

As I stood by the main entrance, busloads of tourists made their way in, clicking photos, commenting, and looking in all directions out of curiosity. I allowed the crowd to snake its way into the temple while I waited outside. I pulled up information on my phone about the temple and learnt more.

Man and Mo are Gods of literature and war respectively. Outside the temple's main entrance, I saw four plaques. The first was dedicated to Man and the second to Mo. The third plaque requested visitors to be silent and respectful of the temple. The fourth plaque asked menstruating women to keep off the main temple hall. I found this last plaque surprising considering that Buddhism holds a remarkably pragmatic view on ritual bodily cleanliness and its relation to spirituality. I wondered if this could be an influence of Hindu traditions from many centuries ago.

The temple was constructed by wealthy Chinese merchants in 1847 during the Qing Dynasty, and it was used as a place to settle disputes. The temple has a dedicated mediation room. It is believed that oaths were taken here accompanied by the ritual beheading of roosters.

One room was dedicated to the gods of literature. The carved idols sat in a row, each holding a book and pen. The room was a library with ancient scriptures and books on display. I walked into these rooms while I waited for the tourist crowds to recede in the main hall so that I could get some quiet time.

The energy in the main hall was ethereal, of another world. It had much to do with the smoke hanging mid-air, almost stationary. I was walking through a curtain of fog, a misty wonderland synonymous with secrets folded into their sheets of smoke.

The smoke emanated from inverted spiral incense coils that hung from the ceiling. I overheard a Caucasian tourist say that the inverted incense coils that hung like lamps would burn for two weeks each before they were replaced with new ones.

A larger-than-life-size brass pen, which was about three feet high, and a brass sword of about the same size each was placed before the main idols of Man and Mo to represent literature and war. Devotees stood before the idols holding incense sticks and praying fervently for wish fulfilment. I saw some visitors write their wishes and tie them into their offerings of fruits, cola, chocolates, biscuits, and just about any food from the supermarket.

I have seen many Hindu temples across India dedicated to different human needs. There is the famous Traffic Ganesha that blesses new vehicles, the US visa-granting Venkateswara, and the Brahma Baba Temple that takes clocks as offering in exchange for speedy wish fulfilment. This was the first time I was seeing deities outside of the Hindu pantheon dedicated to specific aspects of life. The Gods of Literature and War were tributes to creative expression and motivation to kill our inner demons.

I sat on a wooden bench on the side of the hall with my gaze fixed on the incense smoke rising up and filling the room in a dreamy haze.

When another busload of tourists started to enter the temple, I walked out of the main hall to see the other parts of the temple. A fortune teller beckoned me to have my future read but I smiled and waved walking by.

The adjacent temple hall was dedicated to many other gods of Taoism and Buddhism where devotees were burning incense sticks and praying with eyes closed and hands folded.

I stepped outside the temple and walked to a park across the street where an old man was feeding the pigeons. I sat for a long time observing the comfort of the pigeons around this man who had visibly built a long and trusting relationship with the birds. This seemed to be their daily ritual.

When I looked around the quiet streets, the peaceful trees, and the chirping birds, I saw such a starkly opposite Hong Kong from the one I had seen the previous day. I couldn't believe that I was in the same city. It had such a different vibe only a short distance away from the centre. I had found this cocoon of calm in the world's epicentre of materialism.

In a short few hours, I had seen how a strong external environment can influence our internal world. I was responding to my immediate surroundings while noticing how they were affecting my senses. I sought quiet places, so I dismissed the role played by busy centres of commerce.

It is said, and I believe, that we see the world as we are. I had set up a challenging task for Hong Kong to show me a side of her that would inspire a specific emotion. Now is it the city's fault that she is much more than just that one emotion I was in the mood for on that day?

The city showed me all that she is, and in the sifting of what I liked and didn't like, I was judging Hong Kong rather harshly.

The fault was not in the city but in me. I had set up an automatic filter to find something specific in the city. Even though this filter was based on a combination of what I already knew of the city and what I wanted to experience, my likes and dislikes stemmed from bite-sized experiences that would go into my memory file of the city for years to come.

If what is inside me is also what I see and feel reflected around me, I am more likely to agree with the place and take back pleasant memories from it. But travel is so much more than liking a place or agreeing with it. My best travel experiences have been the ones that question what I always believed while leaving me with memories that would serve my mind in new and interesting ways.

It is about the outer environment making changes to the inner world rather than the inner world pre-deciding what the outer world should be like for it to be accepted and liked. It was necessary for me to see the two sides of Hong Kong to unravel this approach to travel.

When yet another busload of tourists arrived, I decided to leave the Man Mo Temple. I carried my introspective mood into the day as I sat at a pub down the street from the temple and ordered green tea while I wrote, inspired by the gods of literature.

Towards evening, I took the subway back into the chaos of Tsim Sha Tsui, but the inner calm stayed with me for a long time. This time, I didn't cringe at the noise, crowd, greed, and gluttony. They didn't affect me as much, perhaps, because I went with an open mind and greater acceptance.

I found a massage parlour and got my legs kneaded to remove the day's accumulated walking stress. A white cat sat next to me as though we were long-lost friends, maybe we were.

When I returned the second time to Hong Kong in two weeks on my way back from Canada, I went to the same places on the waterfront and walked down the now-familiar streets. The noise, people, and the crowded energy of the place didn't leave me rattled as it had the first time.

I knew the streets now. We were like acquaintances getting to know each other better. I even had a favourite bench on the waterfront and I knew where I wanted to eat. I had found my calm, and I was also aware of the chaos. I wasn't going to let either decide how I felt inside.

My experience of Hong Kong made me take a pause while reflecting on my expectations from the places I visited. As I am about to arrive at a new place, a few minutes into landing at the airport or a few kilometres outside the city train junction, I give the place carte blanche. That is how I allow the place to talk to me in its own language. If I don't understand it, it is my problem.

17

Feminine Keepers of Faith in India Guard the Path Ahead with their Light

The dried leaves crunched under my feet as I walked deep into the forest amid the wilderness. The sunlight was bright but not harsh as it filtered through the dense foliage. The air was cool, but I felt warmth rising from my belly as I walked further into the forest carrying two bags containing all the items needed to perform a fire ritual.

I was walking to the Goddess temple in Naidupuram, up in the hills seven kilometres from Kodaikanal town in South India. The temple was consecrated by the locals to represent the Pleiades constellation. Seven stones in their natural form were erected in a row to represent the seven sisters' association of the Pleiades in Greek mythology.

The story goes that Titan Atlas was forced to hold up the sky for eternity. When Orion had evil intentions for his seven daughters, the Pleiades, Atlas was unable to protect them. In came Zeus, who turned them into stars so Orion would not be able to harm them.

The Pleiades, in Taurus constellation, called *Krittika nakshatra* in Sanskrit, make up the brightest cluster of stars. They represent new beginnings and hold great significance for the farming community especially during harvest time.

In Hindu mythology, the ruling deity of the Pleiades is believed to be the Fire God Agni. They also represent the victorious rising sun, again, the fire energy.

Mirroring the Pleiades up above stood seven stones in this forest representing the seven sisters, which in turn represent the power of feminine divinity. I was going to perform my first fire ritual, an initiation of sorts, at this sacred place in nature with the Pleiades for witness.

I laid out all the accoutrements of religious ritual and, with a deep breath, started the chants. As the fire rose, taking my intentions up above to the Pleiades, I felt one with the divine feminine, nurturer, protector, and giver of life, and the embodiment of existence itself.

I believed in her power, which made this ritual extra special for me. It was the start to a lifetime of understanding the Devi (Goddess) in me as well as around me. This one ritual transformed the way I would look at fire and femininity and the strong connection between the two.

Over the years, I visited powerful divine centres representing the feminine energy. I believe that my first-ever fire ceremony established a deep personal relationship with the feminine in the universe. When life took me to places where the Devi shone in her sparkling brilliance, I was in awe. At the heart of this experience is faith, a deep knowing that she is there in me and all around me, too.

These are only a few different avatars of her force and influence in the lives of believers.

Seeking Justice at Arulmigu Masani Amman Temple, Pollachi

I sat cross-legged, back straight, gaze fixed on the ten-inch-tall black idol of Goddess Masani in interior Tamil Nadu. The temple hall reverberated to the sounds of roaring drumbeats and cymbals, their echoes overlapping and bouncing off the walls, piercing my ears and creating a vacuum in that space and time where nothing else existed.

I was in an almost-trance, unable to take my eyes off the idol that was being bathed in oil, sandal paste, turmeric, red kumkum powder, flowers, and water. The ritual, called *abhishekam, lasted about forty minutes, during which I* barely blinked or moved, but I felt intense heat rising up my lower back. I touched my back to feel if something other than my saree grazed my skin, but I only felt damp sweat clinging to my body.

Standing on the edge of the Anaimalai Forest at the base of the hills near the Aliyar River, this ancient temple is unusual in many ways. The presiding deity, Masani Devi or Masani Amman, is in a lying posture, while most goddess idols worshipped in temples are seated or standing. Large at fifteen feet tall, the Goddess has four hands, each holding a drum, snake, trident, and skull.

This is the temple of justice, where believers grind red chillies and offer the paste to the idol in the faith that she takes away injustices, ill-health, and obstacles. Women with menstruation irregularities visit to pray for healthy cycles.

The story of the Goddess is rooted in a great tragedy that led to her unjust killing. She was falsely accused of stealing a mango from the king's orchard and was sentenced to death, although she pleaded innocence. She now takes the form of an exalted goddess to help believers who are unfairly punished either through the law or through karma leading to them losing wealth, status, fame, and respect for reasons known or unknown.

When I entered the temple as a curious visitor from the city, eager priests doled out instructions on removing the evil eye on me by grinding red chillies. I took a handful of red chillies, poured them at the base of the grinding stone and turned the heavy stone clockwise to crush the chilies.

Then I collected the red chili paste with my bare hands and smeared it on the stone idol of the Goddess, right beside the grinding stone.

'All your worries are now over,' a priest declared, and then asked me to return to the temple in ninety days to bathe the Goddess in oil as a way to thank her. I did return in three months, not out of fear but as a completion of the cycle, respect, and gratitude for those energies unknown to me but working in my favour.

As I sat to watch the Goddess's oil bath ritual, I felt an inexplicable vibration through my body, which I didn't want to probe further. I stayed with the feeling of calm in my heart and thoughtlessness in my mind. It was an all-knowing and not-worrying feeling of evenness that stayed with me for a long time after I had left the temple.

Ranganath, the taxi driver who drove me to the airport, was at first incredulous that I travelled alone. He asked if I had family in Coimbatore and if I was visiting the temple on my own. He looked at me with great curiosity as a woman who was out in the world outside the safety of family and socially approved male company. Over the course of our conversation, he gradually accepted that I am a solo woman traveller, I pay my own bills, and will board a flight without company.

He spoke no English but still continued to ask questions using gestures and single words in English, Hindi and Tamil.

'Marriage?'

'Family?'

'Work?'

'Salary?'

We somehow got on with the conversation and continued

to talk as we ate at a roadside restaurant. I saw that I had given him much to ponder. He looked at me with curious eyes as though he had many more unanswered questions about how it was even possible for a woman to be out by herself.

'Your father allowed you to travel alone?' he blurted out.

'Yes,' I simply replied. He wanted to ask more questions about my father's thinking in all this but did not. Every woman is only seen in relation to a man. She is someone's daughter or wife or mother, and rarely ever just a woman standing on her own, living life as she pleases. That, still, is a rarity in many parts of interior India.

This is the land where extraordinary circumstances could elevate a woman on the street to the status of a goddess. When we enter the temple, the goddess is seen as all-powerful and all-knowing, an energy that is beyond the reach of the common human.

The believer may imbibe elements of this feminine divinity in understanding and engaging with the goddess in her. A believer trusts that she can awaken the latent divine energy already present.

Centres that hold such power can set off the process in the form of intense experiences. But all this happens only if we believe.

The taxi driver believed that the feminine power was confined to the stone deity within the temple. He did not see it expressed in believers who had awakened that energy in them around him. But if a woman believes that her power goes with her everywhere she goes, it is worth thinking about the expansive greatness that could achieve.

Devis Commune with Nature at Chausathi Yogini Temple, Odisha

The power of faith is best witnessed at an Indian temple festival. I witnessed this at Bhubaneswar in July as millions of pilgrims and tourists from around the world descended on this eastern Indian city for the annual Jagannatha Temple festival, in which the three sibling-gods, Krishna, Balaram, and their sister Subdhadra, come out of their sacrosanctum for a chariot ride.

I was conned at temple visits, overcharged everywhere, and emotionally blackmailed into buying sacred prayer articles. There was dust, grime, and too many people in the markets; and the beach at Puri was brimming with pilgrims such that I couldn't walk anywhere near the water. I hired an autorickshaw and rode out of the city, across quiet farm fields and through clean air.

The calm of the village roads, barely minutes outside the hustle and bustle of Bhubaneswar, was soothing. I stopped on the banks of the Bhargavi River in Hirapur, an easy twenty-minute ride from central Bhubaneswar, to visit one of the only four surviving Chausathi Yogini temples in the world. This was an open-air temple sitting in the lap of nature, carrying all the power of the divine feminine.

Chausathi, in Odiya, translates to sixty-four.

'This temple was built in the 9th century by Queen Hiradevi of the Bhauma Dynasty to represent the sixty-four incarnations of Goddess Durga or Shakthi,' the guidebook read.

Only eight feet high, the entrance was a curved stone wall with carvings that had lost their sharp edges and definition to the elements of rain and wind over the ages.

I entered the temple and walked through a pathway with stone statues lined up every few feet on either side, all open to the sky. This was an open-air temple, standing one with all the five elements of nature, the Bhumandala of earth, water, fire, air, and space.

I walked through the main circular structure, pausing at each of the sixty-four beautifully carved sensuous representations of the Goddess—as musicians, dancers, and fierce huntresses wielding bows and arrows. Each sculpture sat in a cavity in the wall specially carved to showcase the Goddess' many forms, each tastefully decorated with anklets, bangles, bracelets, garlands, earrings, necklaces, and other ornaments.

I closed my eyes and could hear the clinking of heavy anklets as dancers paid obeisance to these marvellous goddesses through movement and artful expression. At the centre of this circle, on a raised platform, was a gloriously beautiful and tall Goddess Kali or Mahamaya. Below her feet lay a human head while the Goddess looked resplendent in her forceful energy and confidence. Her avatar reminded me of the eternal victory of good over evil.

Every village in Odisha has a Gram Devi or a village chief deity, and this temple is believed to be a representation of all the Gram Devis of the state, following the mixed culture of Tantric Hinduism and Tantric Buddhism.

On this lazy cloudy monsoon afternoon, a gentle breeze created ripples on the river. Standing amid sixty-four black granite idols of Goddess Durga was a deeply powerful and personal experience for me. I knew that words would render inadequate the emotion of feeling one with nature in an open-to-the-elements temple, where the feminine force exposed all her energy without fear of ruination. And she continues to stand strong since the 9th century.

The guidebook also mentioned that the Yoginis in this temple were still worshipped by the locals of Hirapur, but I didn't find any signs of daily worship. As in other temples, there was no priest or even a donation box for offerings.

As I made my way back the pathway closer to the exit, two men who looked like government officials walked into the temple.

One man asked, 'Who told you about this temple?'

I answered, 'The guidebook.'

'And you just came to have a look?' he seemed surprised that I would be so trusting of a guidebook.

'Yes,' I shrugged.

'People rarely come here,' he commented.

I spent more time looking at the sculptures, eavesdropping on his conversation with his associate about restoring a sculpture that he was pointing to. These may be ancient stones that deserve preservation, but it is the energy these sculptures awaken in us that inspires the art of living.

I walked out into the waiting autorickshaw to head to another temple, which was large and thronging with pilgrims. I had danced with the goddess energy in this empty temple. With a smile on my lips, I visited the other places of importance knowing that this goddess would continue to dance in me wherever I went.

The Lure of Instant Wish-Fulfilment at Sri Nimishambha Temple, Karnataka

The cow mooed lazily when I walked into the front yard of the two-room house. Chickens chased each other around and sarees hanging to dry from a clothesline fluttered in the breeze.

'Who is it?' a woman asked in Kannada, peeping out the half-open door.

'I'm here to see Panditji,' I replied, using the common name for a priest.

'He will be here in a few minutes. He has gone out. Please wait here,' she said, pointing to a stone bench by the main door. I sat and waited.

Not much later, the priest rode a scooter into the yard, his son standing in the space between the handle and seat.

'Hello!' he smiled and beckoned me inside.

I sat cross-legged on a straw mat while the priest brought out a wooden floor desk and cowrie shells. He took a deep breath, closed his eyes, held the conch shells in his closed fist, and let the shells drop on the desk like rolling the dice. He studied the shells for a few minutes and separated them into groups of four. I looked for a pattern but couldn't find one.

He looked at me, smiled, and then revealed why I was there and what questions I had in mind. He was accurate, and this prompted me to ask more questions. The priest was good at answering polar questions of 'yes, no, and maybe' but was limited by language and his exposure to advanced urban lifestyles to answer open-ended questions or delve deeper into problem-solving. Still, it was fascinating to meet one of the few astrologers who practised conch-shell divination.

'Many people openly condemn this practice but secretly come to me. They feel that just because they are literate, they aren't supposed to believe anymore in these age-old traditions,' he said.

'Put all these questions aside. Whatever has to happen will happen. Go to Nimishamba Devi and ask Her to take care of everything. Make a special prayer for the Sri Chakra in the *Garbhagudi* (sanctum sanctorum). And carry lemons for the Goddess,' he said, and sent me away with a smile.

The short two-km drive from the priest's house in Srirangapatna town took me through winding roads to Ganjam Village by the Kaveri River. The majestic seven-storey temple stood tall and imposing over the dry and sleepy village. Just metres away from the temple steps, the river flowed gently, hopping and dancing over submerged rocks. The mid-morning summer heat didn't deter the female devotees—there were more women than men—queuing up in silk sarees and their best gold jewellery.

The crowd on that day was considered lean, and I got my first glimpse of the Goddess twenty minutes after I joined the queue. Carved in black stone, and with only the faint yellow light of an oil lamp in the sanctum reflecting off her face, the idol looked radiant and powerful. Her diamond nose ring glistened against her black skin, and her large eyes shone with a knowing spark. She wore a rich, green silk saree with a bright red border that shone bright.

Inside the sanctum also sat the Sri Chakra, a metal device made of nine interlocking triangles around a central point, which locks mystical energy. The Sri Chakra is used in the worship of primordial energy that carries the blueprint of all creation. The Sri Chakra, also carved of the same black stone as the idol in the sanctum, was covered in flowers. I gave the lemons that I had bought outside the temple to the priest, who kept them on the Sri Chakra. He then offered the flowers and chanted mantras.

Nimisha means minute. The Goddess sitting in this 400-year-old temple built by Mummadi Krishnaraja Wodeyar, Maharaja of Mysore, is said to grant wishes and resolve issues within a minute. It is with this unwavering faith that devotees flock to the temple.

The temple's specialty is to grant the marriage boon to unmarried girls, and babies to women wanting to conceive. The Goddess is the avatar of Parvathi. And where there's Parvathi, can Lord Shiva be far behind? There are shrines dedicated to Lord Shiva, Ganesha and Anjaneya within the temple.

The priest returned the lemons to me and asked me to keep them at the altar in my house for a few days and offer them to a flowing river, or squeeze the lemon juice and drink up. I did the latter.

Walking out of the temple, I sat by the river, watching a bunch of children have a splashing good time in the water, and thought about the cycle of making and granting wishes. There can never be clear answers to wish fulfilment, and where and how our deepest desires come true. But we continue to wish anyway, simply because we believe. It is also how the cycle of life carries on. And to turn this business up a notch, not too far from the Nimishamba Temple, sits the Kshanambika Temple. *Kshana* means second. The promise of instant wish fulfilment gets a whole new relevance in this high-speed era. Now it depends whether you believe that your wishes will be fulfilled in a minute or in only a second.

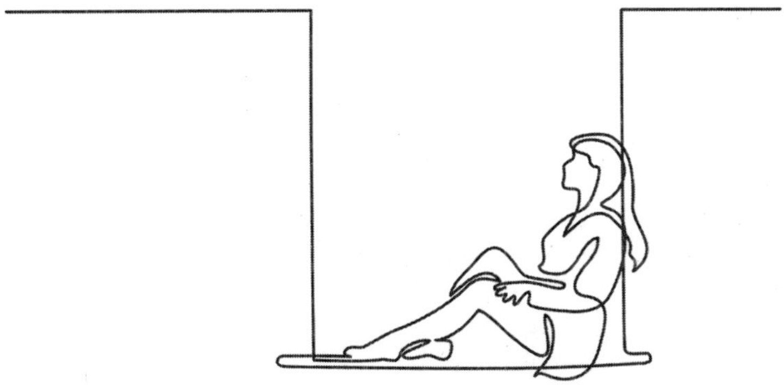

I HEAL

I travelled to these places not seeking to heal but I healed anyway. These travels were a karmic calling, inviting me to their mystical haven where I could be vulnerable to heal, repair, and restore.

18

Egg Rolling towards Soulful Peace in the Squamish Rainforest

Nikita held an egg and pressed it all over my body. She ran the egg over each breast, slid it along my waist, my nether regions, my back, my shoulders, and my womb. She was applying pressure on the egg and pressing it against my body with much force. I was surprised that the egg didn't break. While she was doing this, I was instructed to look straight into Becky's eyes. Becky was standing about four feet in front of me and looking into my eyes unblinkingly.

'Do not at any point look down or look up. Don't look away from Becky's eyes,' Nikita had told me. This, she explained, was to prevent my consciousness from escaping the moment. Looking downward would take my body back into an old trauma, and looking up would mean that my soul is escaping my body unable to bear the trauma. I had to work with the trauma and through it to emerge on the other side. This could only happen if I stayed in the moment.

At the start of this ritual, Nikita drew a line on the ground with a stick.

'First, I will do the egg ritual. Becky will break the egg on Bone Mother, who will take away your pain. Then you must cross this threshold. Remember that once you cross this threshold, you are making a promise to continue your spiritual work,' she said. I nodded.

As Nikita ran the egg all over my body, the unexplained grief returned. I did not control the tears. I didn't know the source of so much grief. I let it flow out in the form of tears. Nikita gave the egg to Becky who broke it on the Bone Mother, a stone in the forest decorated and revered by the locals.

'Now, whenever you're ready, cross the threshold,' Nikita said. I crossed the line and stood in front of Becky who enveloped me in a bear hug.

Nikita hugged me from behind and we three women embraced for a long time in an unhurried, familiar, and comforting sisterhood.

Nikita and Becky, two elder shamans, were working on an old grief that they said was stuck in my womb. They sat with me and listened to my symptoms of unexplained grief that had welled up in my body in the course of the last few days. Nikita then described the significance of the simple yet powerful egg-healing technique used in the shamanic tradition to deal with emotional pain.

This ritual took place in the largest rainforest in North America, the Pacific Northwest temperate rainforest, stretching through northwestern USA and the western Canadian coast. We stood in these lush green forests at Squamish town, an hour out of Vancouver in British Columbia, Canada.

We faced an open-air temple that was put together using stones to make a cone-shaped pyramid, about four-feet high. Four large stones—like milestones—were erected in each cardinal direction. This temple under the trees was dedicated to the Bone Mother, the keeper of the water of life and of death; also believed to be the connection to our ancestors and to the spirit world. Colourful ribbons fluttered from the tree branches hanging above the stone pyramid. Flowers and ribbons spilled over from the Bone Mother, too.

I was in this part of the world on a ten-day gathering of shamans. The gathering of about seventy-five included shamanic believers at every level of intensity, from low to fiendish. But the majority displayed mid to high levels of faith and involvement in the tradition. Many were practitioners and healers. Many more were in need of healing. And the others were there to support their leader, Jack.

Jack taught his own school of shamanism, complete with initiation into the tribe, rituals, and ancestral work. The elders of the group trained the apprentices who were then initiated into the tradition in a grand ceremony. Along the way, the aspiring shamans were taught to connect with nature's elements—fire, earth, wind, and water—to become 'guardians' of these elements.

This was all new to me. I had been on a solitary spiritual path with discipline and rigour for over fifteen years, not really meeting anyone else who did this work. I didn't actively seek out to meet others on the path. I didn't feel the need because I strongly believed that important healing happened where the body, mind, and spirit were in tune with the universe. I approached my spiritual journey with the understanding that the most conducive space for my learning was within me, and not in a group.

Emerging from this largely solo journey, I found the gathering dramatic. The conference location was an unused children's camping ground. A tent was erected around the campfire site to create the main conference hall. Jack and the 'ordained initiates' and elders of the shaman community wore colour-coded robes. Red robes meant that they were fire guardians. Blue robes meant that they were water guardians. The initiates wore black.

A group of about 8–10 drummers brought their djembes and other African drums to create a lively atmosphere. We woke up every day to drumming, music, dancing, singing, storytelling, and rituals. The fire, revered as Grandfather Fire, was ritualistically brought to life on the first day of the conference and put to sleep on the last day. Fire guardians were appointed to be on duty round the clock to keep alive the big fire, never allowing it to die.

When there were no sessions in the main hall, the attendees went into break-out sessions to learn the basics and nuances of Tarot card reading, fire walking, capnomancy (divination using smoke), ancestral shamanic work, fire throwing, drum making, Reiki, Five Rhythm trance dance, sound healing, and indigo dyeing.

During the main sessions, where all attendees gathered, Jack and his core team of shamans made ritualistic offerings to the primary altar. From there, we all proceeded to the day's break-out sessions.

I participated in the gathering with the attitude to learn. I wasn't a sceptic, nor was I a blind believer. I went with an open mind willing to observe and deduce my own findings. I immersed in the experiences. But within a few days, my body and mind grew tired. I wanted to be alone and didn't want to share space with so many people all day. Sadness from an unknown source enveloped me.

This sadness grew bigger and bigger till it had consumed me. It bothered me no end that I didn't know the reason for this constant dull ache in my heart. I wondered if this was called depression. Was it what was called past-life residual pain? I had no way of knowing. I felt like I was carrying a heavy stone on my shoulders all the time. Except, this was emotional heaviness, not physical.

One day, when I was talking to Becky, I broke down. I didn't know the reason. I didn't know where the grief was coming from. Becky immediately informed Jack. He came searching for me and found me sitting under a tree weeping for no reason. I experienced a surge of grief. He hugged me and suddenly I felt that heaviness in my heart retreat into a dark, inaccessible corner of my body. Jack embraced me for a few seconds and said that I was experiencing a woman's grief. I didn't ask him what that meant.

He spoke to Nikita and Becky, and they all decided on a plan of action to remove this grief. The pain is showing itself now as it seeks to be released, they said. What followed that evening was the egg ritual in the presence of the Bone Mother.

After the ritual, my heart felt vulnerable. I felt as though I was too transparent, and that people could see all of me. I couldn't feel the heavy emotions but, in its place, I experienced raw vulnerability, still an uncomfortable state of being. I stayed with the feeling and allowed it to settle in time, which it did, in a few weeks.

The energy at the gatherings was intense and heavy. This had nothing to do with the raging fire at the centre of the site. The rituals brought to the surface much potent energy. People felt an entire gamut of emotions from joy and sadness to gratitude, hope, love, and belonging in that room.

One of the participants told me, 'People love each other so much here. They help each other and are so kind and generous and honest. Why can't all of humanity be this way?' All of these sentiments played a palpable role in shifting what every participant experienced during the gathering.

Powerful healers had gathered in that room, many perhaps may not have been aware of their own power. These were healers who had waded in the world of unknown dimensions of the mind and consciousness without a route map. With no formula and no specific guide to navigating this vast sea of consciousness, they were working by experimentation and sharing from experienced spiritualists and healers.

The shamans had the gift of connecting with different dimensions through meditation and were using that reach to heal and work on better understanding the soul and the eternal spirit. While connecting with unknown parts of the consciousness, it is possible to feel unfamiliar energies and emotions. Many of us felt this in the form of discomfort and instability.

Some participants cried during the sessions. Some others stared at the fire in a trance for a long time. Most were there to forget their immediate reality and its problems and connect with their core self through the power of ceremony and the natural elements. At the heart of these rituals was the fundamental belief that fire, water, earth, and wind were sacred.

None of this was new to me. The Hindu animistic tradition that I had grown up around taught the art of negotiating with the natural elements of fire, wind, water, earth, and other energies. Here, the only difference was the language used. English and Gaelic were the predominant languages used in these ceremonies while the Hindu culture primarily uses Sanskrit.

Meeting Past-Life Connections

In an intriguing ritual one morning, Jack talked about ancestors in past lives and the many souls that have criss-crossed with ours over multiple lifetimes. As he spoke, the drummers created an ethereal ambience with slow and soulful drumbeats, transporting us to a mystical world of fascinating possibilities. Add to that the white vapour emanating from the fire and the incense, lending the gathering a paradisical air.

'Allow the mind to wander untethered to different dimensions, and the names will come to you,' urged Jack. He wore a velvet shiny robe etched with glittering golden embroidery. As he walked by us, he asked us to trust where our mind leads us.

I took a deep breath and did as I was told. I saw people get up from their seats, pick up colourful ice cream sticks laid out on the floor, write on it, lay it by what was growing into a long line of ice cream sticks, and return to their seat or continue walking around the fire.

I sat for a long time, not knowing what I should do. My mind drew a blank. When I flirted at the fringes of my attention seeking an answer, no name came up. I gave up trying rather quickly and was ready to take a short nap to the drumming music. Just as I was drifting into the sleep state, I heard a male voice whisper the name 'Simon' in my right ear.

My eyes opened wide in surprise. I looked around to see if anyone had called out that name or had said anything near me. But there was nobody near me. It was a name calling out to me. I trusted it and wrote it on an ice cream stick to acknowledge this connection even though I knew nothing more.

I started to walk around the fire, and more names were called out in my head. Another name that popped up was Ranga Rao. A third name came up, too—Liu.

I sensed a powerful belonging to someone somewhere during this ritual. I couldn't articulate the emotion. It was a mixture of love, longing, desire, and bittersweet joy. I couldn't comprehend who I felt this concoction of emotions for. All I knew was that what I felt was real because it came from the depths of my heart.

As it happens with 'energy work'—as it is popularly called—the difficulty is often in dealing with ambiguity. I didn't know who these people were: Simon, Ranga Rao, and Liu. I was unlikely to get my answers immediately. It was highly likely that I would never get my answers in the way that I wanted at a time that I desired. And I should be comfortable with not knowing for the most part. This comfort with not knowing is the primary trait to staying balanced while working with unknown dimensions of life.

The more important part of this exercise was to acknowledge how I was feeling at that moment. I could ask myself, *How can I honour these emotions of belonging and longing that have just made themselves known to me?*

If I were keen on making sense of these names and how they connect to me, my mind could make up a story about Simon based on one Simon that I had met in previous years. This connecting of the dots could satiate my need for knowing, but it would just be my logical mind jumping in to explain something in a neat and organised order that was acceptable to me.

It is more challenging to keep an open mind while continuing to explore the world's mysteries, and in reminding ourselves that the only certainty is that nothing is certain.

Similarly, I could not make complete sense of the egg-healing ritual. I approached it with equal parts of trust, mindfulness, and gratitude for the experience. Synchronicity had brought the two elder shamans and me together in that Canadian forest for a reason. I trusted the synchronicity. Worrying about the effectiveness of the ritual would go against the trust that I placed in the universe to bring me the right experiences and people for my growth. I wanted to trust that my body knew how to heal, and that it would reveal the results to me in time.

Trust with a dash of dubiety is a good recipe for navigating vast unknown dimensions that the human mind cannot yet clarify or quantify. Keeping this balance is key to treading dark pathways. A mix of trust and mindfulness is the crucial combination to ensure that a seeker continues progressing on the spiritual path without getting stuck with the first thing that promoted positive change and healing for her.

It is much like being so mesmerised by the first rose that you come across at a flower garden that you fail to see that the garden is full of beautiful flowers of different varieties, colours, fragrances, and at different stages of bloom. Only when you walk across the garden will you get to the other end. Too much blinding trust can be a problem. So can constant doubt or even debilitating scepticism—such as the belief that there is no flower in the world other than a rose.

At the gathering, I saw seekers at every level of the spiritual journey. Some would be comfortable to stay with the rose a little longer before moving ahead in the garden while some others smelled the rose and the jasmine and many other flowers, too. I saw the whole rainbow of seekers, gurus, humanitarians, green activists, lovers, and evolved guides all at different phases of their deeply personal journey.

One such colourful personality was Tim, the tattoo artist. At six-feet tall and any visible skin apart from his face covered in tattoos, Tim made for a conspicuous presence as he walked anywhere across the campsite. With piercingly intense eyes and soft features, Tim was the man-in-demand at the gathering as he was the on-site tattoo artist.

With over thirty years of tattooing experience, I felt safe in Tim's hands. I had never fancied getting a tattoo in all my life. But when I sat on the plane to Canada, I changed my mind and decided to get one. Meeting Tim for the first time made my decision firmer.

Tim attended this conference every year, made tattoos for the attendees, and played the drum at the big gatherings. I spent time with Tim, who I noticed was immersed in the spiritual experience, and yet was able to observe things objectively and step away without judgment.

Tim and I instantly clicked, and I spent time getting to know him. I asked him what motivated him to keep returning to these conferences.

He said, 'I get to meet new people every year. It's a good routine change. I love tattooing wherever I am. And I love drumming. It's all the things that I love.'

I asked him if he has ever felt the urge to deep-dive into the spiritual path and further immerse in it.

'I am immersed in it alright,' he replied, 'I have found my own path where creativity, art, music, and motorcycle riding all intersect to make for a lively spiritual experience. I can hold a conversation about different spiritual paths, but I have never plunged into any one path only, necessarily.'

I realised that Tim had found his flower garden with multiple varieties of flowers and enjoyed the sensory experience that each offered. He had forged his own path.

Another man who expanded my worldview was a Sasquatch descendant. I met Sunbow, a French-Canadian shaman and author of several books about his experiences with Sasquatch sightings. Sasquatch or Yeti or Bigfoot are hairy, bigger-than-human creatures that stay in the wilderness in North America.

It is believed that their DNA is designed differently from the other living creatures on this planet. They are known to exist mainly from the sightings of their footprints stumbled upon by those who wander in the wilderness.

Sunbow was at the conference to talk about his Sasquatch sightings. His first contact with a Sasquatch was in 1983 in the forests of Arizona. He saw a Sasquatch walk and sit 100 feet from him. They're hairy from head to toe, taller than humans in general, he said.

Sunbow said that they are inter-dimensional beings. The image of the Sasquatch looked like a hologram, and they show images to humans through telepathy, he said. There is an unfamiliar feeling that rises when a human first comes in contact with a Sasquatch, he said. In his session, he mentioned that he must be one-twenty-fourth Sasquatch descendant.

That evening, after the last session in the big tent, as the group headed to their respective rooms to retire for the night, Sunbow stepped away from the walking path and stood under a tree. Curious, I stayed behind him and watched. A few owls appeared above his head and flew in circles. A couple of bats flew nearby, and there was movement and sound in the bushes behind where he stood.

It was as though he turned on a switch to call on these animals and they responded to his call. I found this fascinating. He saw me watching him and pointed a finger up to one owl above his head. I saw that owl fly away.

For the first time, I saw what it was like to be completely one with nature and most at home in the company of animals. What's more, the animals felt at home with him, too.

The next day, one of the facilitators, Qyunn, hosted a breakout session to remember the witch in each of us. She spoke of the Salem witch trials, the Spanish Inquisition, and many such trials through history that targeted those who practiced witchcraft.

'Every one of us carries some part of that trauma of witch burning and execution; and even the trauma of not being allowed to follow our intuition to live in a way that flows most naturally to us. This session is about remembering that part of our soul and releasing that trauma,' she said.

A group of twenty participants sat in a dark room with curtains drawn, and almost no light seeping in.

'Keep your eyes closed for the duration of the session. This is going to be a sensory experience in which I will pass around certain objects, which are likely to trigger some past-life memories. Keep silent through the session and check in with your own body and emotions when you hold these objects in your hand,' Qyunn instructed.

The group had figured out a way to pass around the objects without dropping them or opening our eyes. We passed around a burning candle, a bowl of water, a heavy lock and key, a rope, a piece of cloth, an iron link chain, a brick, and some other items.

These objects served as reminders of the abuses of those who were even suspected of pursuing witchcraft. The objects were reminders of trials by fire, drowning, being locked up, tied up in chains, buried alive, and many other forms of execution.

The energy in the room grew intense and serious, and once the lights came on there was thick silence for a few minutes. Every participant shared his/her experience. Some cried and said that they had connected with a deep part of their spirit through this simple yet powerful exercise.

I felt a shiver when I kept my hand in the bowl of water. The clicking of the lock and key was a familiar sound. Terror and fear welled up deep within me when I heard the click. I was unsettled by the experience and was happy to step out in the company of trees.

We each then found a tree or a plant or a corner in nature and connected in a way that was personal and intimate. We were asked to release the trauma and transmute it into a positive story of transcending a circumstance.

Something important was released during that session and at various points throughout the gathering, I felt. Many instances of any shift within my spirit may have even bypassed my conscious mind.

Did I have to go all the way to a Canadian forest for these experiences? I believe so. It was not because the place offered the best spiritual experience. It was because at that moment, I was destined to be there, heal in exactly the manner that I did, and proceed with my spiritual life using the experiences at that gathering. For that, I had to go there and nowhere else.

It reminds me again of what my teacher keeps telling me: You are exactly where you are supposed to be, doing exactly what you are doing, and feeling exactly what you feel right now. So, trying to imagine that you needed to be elsewhere on another path is only anxiety-inducing and a pointless thought.

I was grateful for every experience, the ones that made me comfortable as well as the ones that increased my discomfort. The gathering was a reminder of my sensitive spirit. It showed me that I was alive. It assured me that I was strong enough to open myself to new experiences. And that in itself was enough.

19

Spirits Rest and Revel in Kodaikanal

My stomach protested the side-to-side swaying at every turn as the bus groaned and creaked its way up the winding hill roads. My body was asking for stillness, no movement, and found relief only when I got off the bus to inhale the cold mountain air while taking in the view of the verdant hills all around.

From here, it was another fifteen-minute ride to the Seven Sisters Farm in Naidupuram, deep in the valley of Kodaikanal, known as the 'princess of the hills' in South India.

At 2,000 metres above sea level, Kodaikanal sits in the Palani mountain range of the Western Ghats and is a refreshing oasis of cool in Tamil Nadu. The hill-town is built around the star-shaped manmade lake on the shores of which the old-moneyed film stars, and politicians own luxurious holiday homes. The town is increasingly gaining popularity as a spiritual seat and a centre for environmental activism.

I rode on the sloping roads, through villages and farms, with stunning views of the blue sky and green earth meeting in the distant horizon. The two-acre farm was everything that I had imagined it to be. A smattering of English-style cottages spread out across the land, pear trees standing pretty on the sloping hillocks, a stream flowing gently and its trickles echoing from one edge of the land, giant goldfish swimming about in a natural pond, and the land overlooking a valley of green covered in eucalyptus trees of the famed Nilgiris oil, evocative of the pungent perfume that both stimulates and heals.

My host, Dev, was warm and welcoming, funny, and observant. He had a small frame and scrawny appearance, his skin clinging tight to his bones and nerves. He looked like he could see beyond the obvious; he seemed to have a rare prescience of the change to come in people's lives. He spoke about energy as though he could talk to it and will it to do things for him. This quality, perhaps, is what made him a sought-after Reiki healer in known circles. He liked to live away from the spotlight, like a hermit most happy in his own company.

I was there to experience the uniquely designed healing programmes that he offered in the most informal resort-like setting. His typical client was a corporate employee who had accumulated years of stress and was now burning out while running out of options and clarity. Dev offered them a way out with his fresh life perspective coupled with Reiki healing that worked on the physical, mental, and astral bodies.

Dev took on only one client at a time, offering his undivided energy and attention. When I visited the farm, a Dutch man in his mid-fifties was on the last leg of his three-week course. I kept out of the gentleman's way as he was processing big internal and external changes while on the programme. I kept to myself, reading, staring at the wonderful view, eating pears, walking around the farm, and enjoying the sounds of birds and farm animals.

I slept in an octagonal-shaped cottage with a wooden pyramid dome. When I laid down in bed, I could see all eight sides of the pyramid rising high up.

'This is great for energy flow. Notice how you will sleep better in this *Ashtakona* room,' Dev said, when I asked him about the inspiration for the cottage design.

Ashtakona is 'octagonal' in Sanskrit. I did sleep well, feeling well rested and with a calmer mind that wasn't racing with thoughts when I woke up.

On the evening the Dutchman left, Dev, Aditi—another visitor from Bangalore—and I sat by the fireplace post dinner. It was pitch-black outside on a new moon night, and we had only the dim light from a floor lamp softly illuminating a part of the room while much of the yellow light came from the crackling fire.

The conversation veered towards supernatural entities, spirits and the popular game of Planchet, also called Ouija or the spirit board.

Dev spontaneously said, 'Let's play,' and found a brown cardboard sheet on which he wrote the English alphabet, numbers from zero to nine, and two options, 'Yes' and 'No'. A planchet is a metal disk placed on the Ouija board, for which we used a coin. Aditi and I followed Dev's lead and placed the right index finger on the coin.

'Close your eyes and concentrate,' he said. We obeyed with equal parts excitement and nervous anticipation.

'Are there any spirits passing by? Would you like to come and talk to us?' he asked loudly to no one in particular. Eyes still closed, I tried to feel any change around me but sensed nothing for a long time. I opened my right eye, just a wink, but saw nothing amiss either.

The tip of my right index finger, which rested on the coin, now moved slightly as the coin started to move. Opening my eyes to see if this was really happening, I found that Dev and Aditi were also staring at the coin. The coin gently slid sideways and stopped. It moved again and stopped.

Dev took a deep breath and asked loudly, 'Are you willing to talk to us?' There was silence for a few seconds and the coin moved in rapid and random directions, darting from east to west and making circles before abruptly stopping.

'We need only one spirit talking to us. Will the others please leave?' he said. There was silence and the coin didn't move.

'Tell us your name, please,' he asked, to which the coin first moved in all directions and then in a slow and deliberate manner moved across the alphabet on the Ouija board, stopping at one alphabet briefly. It stopped at G, then A, B, R, I, E, and L.

'Gabriel?' I asked. There was silence and the coin didn't move.

I watched carefully this time to see who among the two, Dev or Aditi, was controlling the coin, but I couldn't tell. We were playing a game here, so I played along.

Dev started to ask questions and the coin responded, using the board.

'Where are you coming from?'

'Jupiter.'

'Why are you here?'

'To see family.'

'Are you Indian?'

'Ha ha.'

'Are you male or female?'

'F.'

This went on for a few minutes before I asked questions about me that only I knew in the room. I noticed that the moment I spoke, the coin movement changed. It became rapid, haphazard, and erratic.

'Where is my childhood home?' I asked.

The coin moved and stopped in a way that could suggest many alphabets at once. I knew for certain that either Dev or Aditi was playing. I asked other questions about people, and important life incidents to which only I would know the answer. The coin movement was aggressive and aimless but it did make a few good guesses.

Aditi asked a set of questions and was surprised that the answers were accurate. This made me believe that it was she who controlled the coin. We were at this game for some time till we ran out of questions. The deathly silence was occasionally interrupted by the crackling fire and the crickets outside.

As we sat staring at the fire, surrendering to the stillness of the night, suddenly, a strong gust of wind blew into the cottage. The doors and windows responded with loud rattling. We heard something break, a cracking sound, by the back door. I could now smell fear in the room as Dev and Aditi looked equally uncertain.

Dev took charge of the moment and said loudly, 'Thank you, Gabriel, for being with us for these moments. Please continue on your journey in this dimension. And please take your friends, if there are any around here, with you. Please clear this place completely and leave.'

We looked around and heard nothing.

Dev sighed and asked if anyone wanted more coffee. Aditi said she would like a cup, and asked, 'Do you think this was true? Did something really happen?'

Dev didn't answer, and I simply shrugged. Dev opened the back door that led to the garden and walked to the small arch under the steps leading to the street. The space under the arch was decorated like a Zen Garden, with terracotta figurines and succulents.

A woman's figurine lay there, broken. He picked it up and examined the cut right at the waist of this ornately decorated voluptuous figure of an Indian woman carrying a pot of water. 'Kaveri,' he said, pointing the broken figurine towards me, referring to her name.

'How do you think it broke? The wind?' I asked.

'Yes. But that's unusual because it is always windy here. It has not affected any of the other figurines,' he said.

'Do you think something actually came and broke it? Some strong energy, perhaps?' I asked, hesitatingly.

He looked at the broken figurine in his hand for a full minute, deep in thought. He was concerned but didn't voice it.

'Maybe. Who knows?' he suddenly dismissed it and walked inside the cottage to make coffee.

We spoke about the erratic movement of the coin on the Ouija board but neither Dev nor Aditi admitted to controlling it. I let it go, preparing to classify this experience as an 'unknown,' an unresolved mystery. I did not want to venture down this dark path of painting an uncertain experience with certainty. If I did, I would always be lying to myself.

We drank coffee in silence, ignoring the elephant in the room. Dev suggested that we go for a drive by the lake. Aditi enthusiastically stood up to leave. 'Isn't it too late?' I asked.

'You can see the lake by night. It will be quiet and serene without all the vacationers and boats on the lake,' Dev replied. So, we headed out.

On the drive, Dev shared stories of unnatural happenings in different parts of Kodaikanal. He mentioned Bryant's Bridge, which was a twenty-minute drive down the hill on the way to the foothills. Dev said that people reported strange incidents like something tugging at them, hearing unusual sounds, and smelling unfamiliar scents. We stopped the car at Bryant's Bridge, which was at a curve on the narrow mountain road and got out to walk about in the dead of night.

I didn't know what to expect—whether I was supposed to hear or feel anything, or simply wait for something to happen. We lingered for a few minutes. Nothing happened. As we drove back to the cottage, Dev continued to share more stories about the bridge as an urban lore of supernatural events.

The next afternoon, I went to the main town of Kodaikanal and took in the atmosphere of tourists exploring the streets and locals going about their business. A toothless, wrinkled old woman gave me a broad smile and stretched out her right palm, asking for alms.

Dev walked up behind me and spoke to her in Tamil, while she responded in a flurry of long sentences with an aggressive tone. Dev placed a few folded currency notes in her hand, and she walked away. This exchange seemed practised. It wasn't the first time this was happening with either the old woman or Dev.

I rented a cycle and pedalled around the lake in the pleasant mid-morning air, passing by rows of shops and eager tourists. When I stopped at a point to click photos, a young boy, not older than sixteen years, wearing a traditional dhoti with white ash smeared on his forehead, approached me and said that he was a palmist. Curious, I asked him to read my palm. He studied the lines on my left palm for a few seconds and shook his head as though he was disappointed at a deep misfortune.

'Mistake happened,' he said, shaking his head.

'What mistake?' I asked, curious.

'By mistake you are born a girl. You should be a boy,' he said in broken English, followed by a few words of Tamil that I did not understand.

I was not sure how I felt about his comment on my gender. So, I laughed and said, 'Too bad. What's done is done now. Nothing can be done to fix it.'

He stared at me with a bit of disappointment, not even attempting to understand what I was saying. He continued to read my palm and made general comments about everything in my life going well, and that I will be happy and healthy always. I thanked him and paid up.

'Who taught you palmistry?' I asked him.

'Everyone in my home reads. Family career,' he replied. He lived in Palani, a few hours across the hills from Kodaikanal, and took the bus daily to catch tourists wandering around the lake.

When I told Dev about the palmist, he said that many such palmists work around the lake, and they sometimes do a good job of telling you just what you need to know at the right time in your life.

'A strong intuition runs in their bloodline, and they don't need to rely on education or logic to activate that intuition,' he said.

I again asked him what had been lingering on my mind, 'How do you think the figurine broke last night?'

'It was strange, but I didn't want to say anything at night and alarm you two. There was definitely some thick and heavy energy that passed by as we played planchet. On its way out, the figurine broke. It was a message, but I don't know the meaning yet. These things happen. You just need to observe and let go. The answers will come to you eventually,' he said.

'You controlled the coin during the game, didn't you?' I asked.

He said that he did initially, but beyond a point, something went out of his control. That's when the figurine broke. So, he decided to stop the game.

I had so many questions: Did it have anything to do with me, or with any of us? What was this incident trying to tell us? I thought energy was intangible; it can break something for real? Was that what we call a ghost?

Dev told me to slow down and calm down. Wouldn't life be so easy if we had all the answers we wanted when we asked the questions? I told him that I do want to know. I wanted to take a peek into the vast unconsciousness and learn what I could.

In my ways, the first step to my increasing curiosity about inanimate matter was born out of this experience. I took baby steps into learning about the astral body—that which we cannot see but which impacts us in deep ways. A life of continuing learning started here in the mountains.

Almost ten years later, I visited this farm again. This time, I saw the terracotta figurine of Kaveri on Dev's study table. It was still broken but he had arranged the idol to stand erect even though the crack showed.

'How is it that you still have Kaveri? You did not release her into the river as you said you would?' I asked.

Dev replied that Kaveri had many more stories and experiences to share.

'She stands here like Sakshi, a witness to all that happens here. She may be broken but she still has life. She has purpose. I may be the one to give her that purpose. Even so, Sakshi stands here and watches everything.'

I asked if there were more such experiences at the farm like the one we had on the night of 'Gabriel'.

Dev smiled. 'We will talk. It's a long life and we will have many opportunities for sharing. For now, let's get another cup of coffee.'

20

A Room in London that Whispers Secrets

Opportunities that knock on the mind's door can pop up at any place, at any time. When we grab those opportunities, we take huge strides forward to expand our understanding of the world. Even when we don't, choosing to simply observe and stay where we are, we are only preparing for the mind to stretch; we are not necessarily moving backward.

One such experience to test my mind presented itself during my stay in London. Room number 5535 on the third floor of the William Goodenough House international student housing, which was a short walk away from King's Cross station, was my home for a year.

The room met my every imagination of a typical English setting derived primarily from detective novels and spy thrillers set in England. The room was comfortable with a bed by the window, a large wooden desk, a desk lamp, a refrigerator, functional wall shelves, a wardrobe, and a wash area. Over a few weeks, I made this room my home, setting up a corner to make tea, a chair by the window for reading, and another at the desk for work and study.

This being my first time crossing the seas and living in a foreign country, I carried the extra baggage of apprehensions, especially since it had been only a few months since the July London terror attacks. But as time grew more distant from the terror attack memory, I accepted this new home and it accepted me.

When my routine was set and my mind space had cleared for calm and new learning, I grew more sensitive to my environment. At first, I experienced only slight discomfort in the room. I felt a pair of eyes on me. I would look out the window to see if anyone could see me. But the window faced the top of a tree, on which bloomed—in spring—pleasantly pink flowers. And then there was the open sky.

A few days later, I felt unusually warm and cool air as I walked around the room. These were like pockets of air at a temperature different from the rest of the room. This felt odd to me at first. I inspected that the refrigerator was in excellent working condition, not emitting any gas that could be dangerous.

Then I checked the windows again. The same cool air was outside as was inside. But every time I walked at the centre of the room I felt a change in temperature. Surely, there must be an explanation for this, I thought, but moved on when I couldn't think of a reason.

A few more days later, strange nighttime happenings kept me awake. I felt a pair of eyes on me. I also felt pinpricks on my body, mostly on my legs and arms. I would try to shake off the physical sensation by rubbing my skin and pulling up the duvet closer to my body or by shifting my sleep position.

One night, these pinpricks grew painfully uncomfortable. They felt like needles poking my arms and legs. Just as I was drifting to sleep, I saw the image of a tall man standing at the centre of the room looking at me. I screamed and woke up.

I could not make sense of this. Was this my most terrifying nightmare? I felt terror, a private terror that I was too scared to even share with anyone. Not knowing how to manage my fear, I did what I was taught to do as a child. I chanted a Sanskrit prayer and called on the divine for protection. I tried to sleep and this time, just as I was drifting into sleep, I saw a revolving door.

The image of the revolving door was vivid. It was not too large but fit comfortably in the centre of my room. Through that revolving door in motion, I could see the man on and off. He was there sometimes and disappeared before reappearing again. I sat up in bed, switched on the light, walked around the room, opened the window, and let in some cool air. I tried to go back to sleep but couldn't do so.

I went to work fatigued and tired the next morning. Over the next few days, I would stay out of the room for long hours on some pretext or the other. When I couldn't stay awake any longer, I would go straight into the room and dive into bed. To tire out my body so much that I slept out of sheer fatigue was the only way I could get some rest. But this was an impractical idea.

The strange room experiences never stopped. I still felt a pair of eyes on me at times, I still felt warm and cool air, I still heard some strange sounds from the wash basin and windows, and I was still woken up by pinpricks on my skin.

One evening, tired and sleepy, I went to the bar for a well-deserved pint. I joined a group of students at a table. One Indian man, Kartik, was narrating an incident from a previous resident of his room, who was aware of a cat spirit's presence.

'She felt the cat in the room all the time. The cat would jump on the bed and lounge in the room all day,' Kartik said.

'Oh my God! If it were me in that room, I would be so scared,' said a woman in an Austrian accent.

'But that's the thing. This is a century-old building. It's not uncommon to find many such stories with memories and emotions still stuck on its walls, lingering, seeking freedom, perhaps,' he said with a faraway glint in his eyes.

'Did she do anything to get rid of the cat?' I asked, curious to find a solution to my own problem.

'No, she didn't. But then why should she? The cat was probably there before her. The cat wasn't doing anything to harm her, and she didn't either. She just let the cat be, and they coexisted,' he said. 'But she told me that on the last day when she was leaving the room, she addressed the cat and said out loud: "You can come with me if you like." A deathly silence followed. She moved back to Germany and sent me an e-mail that the cat hadn't followed her.'

'Which means the cat's still here?' I asked.

'Maybe. I don't feel anything in the room but then I'm not that sensitive,' he said.

I looked around the table and there sat highly intelligent research scholars and influencers from diverse world cultures and fields of study. They were listening to ideas without judgment, which gave me the courage to share my experience of the man and the revolving door in my room.

They heard me out patiently and weren't surprised. They empathised, nodded, and offered to buy me another pint. But they didn't, at any point, question or doubt what I saw or felt. No solution came of this, but I felt lighter with the sharing. And here lies the power of community.

I no longer felt alone in my predicament of the invisible revolving door. Like the German woman who didn't let the cat affect her life in London, I now felt that it was not cowardly to let the man and the door simply be while I got on with my life. In its own way, this was a solution, too.

When I returned to my room that night, I felt at home. I had a greater acceptance of invisible energies that were beyond my control. I didn't know enough to make sense of it. It could have been a magnesium deficiency that gave me those pinprick-like sensations in my body. My mind could be filtering images from the past of revolving doors, hooded killers standing by the bed with knife in hand, and so on.

My practical intelligence would not allow an over-simplification of my experience, but my gut instinct was strong enough to show me that what I was sensing was not a figment of my imagination. I had to observe and accept everything as it was without allowing fear to take over at any point. I was highly mindful of the possibility of fear controlling my mind. That would be more terrifying than not understanding what I was seeing and feeling.

I decided that in an observant mode I was going to carry on with my life, live, and let live. I would not jump to conclusions. By making space for different experiences without judgment, I was stretching my mind and allowing my consciousness to expand in beautiful ways. This process of expansion itself was healing and giving.

I was telling myself that I was in charge. I was showing myself how to be in charge of my own experiences. This was enough.

Over the course of the next few weeks, a name popped in my head for the man—Richard. The name just came to me out of the blue when I wasn't thinking of the room or the man. Richard let me be. And I let him be. I'd always remember room number 5535 as Richard's room.

When I checked out of this room a year later, I was aware that I was adding to the innumerable stories that these ancient walls carried. And yet these very stories gave the room its character, its lightness of being despite the years of experience.

Six years later, I returned to William Goodenough House on a work visit to London. I sublet a room at the student housing and preferred to stay there rather than at a hotel, with the hope of reviving my fondest London memories.

To my utter disappointment, the building had been completely renovated. The reception no longer had a twentieth-century look with its wall-to-wall wooden pigeonholes for letters. The old-world look had been replaced by swanky steel and glass. The courtyard where I spent hours reading on the wooden bench now had a fancy fountain but no place to sit. There were now elevators in which bright artificial lights bounced off the flashy metal interiors. You could check your appearance on their spotlessly clean surface.

The biggest disappointment of all—there was no room number 5535 anymore. I regretted my decision to revisit the house. The physical symbols of my time there had been altered. But there was a corner in my mind, where these memories were still alive, where they couldn't be touched. Room number 5535 would still be the same in that corner of my mind.

I could still close my eyes and smell the mixed scent of tea, my perfume, pine leaves and spicy dry powdered chutney from home. I could hear the faint hum of the refrigerator and the breeze as it grazed the glass windows. I could still see the bottle green wall-to-wall carpet, the white wardrobe, wooden shelves, bedside table, and the reading lamp. Room number 5535 was still alive for me in every way.

I closed my eyes again and this time I saw the revolving door. Only one question remained: What happened to Richard? Did he manage to find his peace? I trust that I will get that answer when I need to hear it. Till then, I would continue to observe, learn, and be present in every moment and every experience.

21

Tiger's Nest Smiles through the Time Warp

The flight from Kolkata to Paro figures high on my list of the most picturesque and thrilling flights I have ever taken. The aircraft almost grazed the mountains on the sides and flirted with the skies above while kissing the clouds below.

We flew zigzag between mountains and dropped low and zoomed up like a rollercoaster while navigating the Himalayan Mountain ranges. As far as my eyes could see in every direction from the tiny aircraft window, the raw beauty of mountains, trees, and water stretched out in full glory.

I spotted the snow-capped Kanchenjunga towering majestically. The co-passengers around me pulled out the cameras and, for a few minutes, all I could hear was the incessant click of the camera.

'What? Are you not going to get shots of the mountain?' the man seated next to me asked.

I shrugged and replied that I would rather enjoy this real-time experience than attempt to click photos through the scratched-up windowpane.

My landing at the Paro International Airport was equally spectacular. A strip of land had been painstakingly evened out in this mountainous region to create a runway. The airport terminal was welcoming with its refreshing architectural design that paid tribute to Bhutanese culture. There was none of the glass, steel, or slanting poles that are a common feature in international airports today. There was no manicured grass, and no flowering bushes to greet travellers. The terminal was a functional and practical white building embellished with carved wood, painted in warm colours atypical of Bhutanese style.

This runway was surrounded by mountains and tall trees. Bhutan didn't have to pretend-create nature because this country knew how to preserve all that is natural. It is one of the only countries in the world where citizens have a constitutional obligation to preserve and protect the environment.

Entering this sort of highly aware and conscious space made me also up-level my mindfulness. I observed everything with more attention, and I wanted to blend into this sacred space.

Immigration was a breeze with no long lines and no tense moments. I also liked that the entire country is a no-smoking zone, so to carry cigarettes into Bhutan one needs to pay a heavy tax. The no-smoking rule which came into effect in 2004 was relaxed a bit in 2012.

The drive out of the airport landed me back again in the lap of nature, this time on the ground. The air was clean, rivers flowed with verve, and the tall fir trees stood like guards protecting the small country.

This was a culture-proud country. Rarely did I see the local Bhutanese wearing denim and t-shirts, the visible symbol of westernisation. Every local, irrespective of age, wore the Gho (for men) and Kira (for women).

The Gho is a knee-length robe tied at the waist by a cloth belt. It has a functional pocket in the front. The men also wear knee-length socks and boots to beat the mountain cold. The Kira consists of a full-sleeved blouse and a wraparound skirt usually in bright colours. The fabric could be thick cotton for daily wear or silk for formal occasions. Although mandated by law since the 17th century to sport the national dress in public, the citizens wore their traditional clothes not out of force but with pride.

I met my local guide, Budha Ching, who was going to be my go-to for all culture-related questions. I saw Budha wear his colourful Gho at all times. Budha became a problem solver, teacher of Bhutanese culture, guide and, in quick time, Facebook friend.

After settling into a cottage in a serene country-style resort surrounded by mountains, I took an easy day of acclimatising. By the second day, I was raring to go on the famed trek to the Tiger's Nest.

Tiger's Nest is a collection of tiny buildings precariously perched on a cliff with a dead drop of 900 feet. It is called the Taktsang Monastery and is one of a kind in the world.

Camera slung over my shoulder, walking shoes laced tight and trekking poles in hand I started this moderately difficult ascent toward the meditation cave in the mountain.

Budha explained, 'This monastery is dedicated to the deity Padmasambhava. This is where he is believed to have meditated for three years, three months, three days, three minutes, and three seconds.'

'Is it true that he rode here atop a tiger?' I asked, recalling the story from my internet research.

'Tigress. Yes. That's why the name,' responded Budha.

The only way to get to the monastery was by foot. A few tourists hired horses to get to almost the very end. The first half of the climb was steep on a wide walking mud path. I took my time adjusting to the path, being aware of the unfamiliar feeling of having reached the edge of the world. Every time I looked out at the mountain peaks and the depths below, I felt I was making a slow ascent towards a magical world of mystery. With the changing landscapes along the way, nature carried on a riveting conversation with me, showing me parts of her, bit by bit.

Every switchback, 180-degree turn on the trail, offered a unique view of the hills and valleys all around. The October sun wasn't harsh and yet gave enough warmth against the cool mountain air.

I was trekking after many months, and I hadn't kept fit due to irregular exercise. But it wasn't my fitness level that bothered me. My left knee began to buckle under pressure. I stopped often to rest the knee.

Besides the knee, another irritation presented itself—my shoelaces kept untying themselves. So, every few minutes I had to stop to tie them back. No matter how tight or differently I tied them they came undone. Budha noticed this and came to my rescue. He taught me to tie my shoelaces in a double knot, which then stayed put.

Budha trekked ahead as the climb grew progressively steeper and more difficult. I was asking every trekker on his way back, 'How much longer to the café?'

Every single trekker would smile and say the same thing, 'Twenty minutes more.'

At some spots along the way, I saw rows of prayer wheels in the middle of the forest. I then saw a temple and a monk who sat in meditation. Why does he sit all the way up here? Then again, why do seekers go all the way to the Himalaya to seek?

A café was set up at exactly the halfway mark to Tiger's Nest. Most trekkers stopped here for tea and a snack. I did, too. Some trekkers would stop here and not continue the rest of the way up.

The group moved in clusters of two and three, clicking, chatting, and panting along the way. I used a trick that a pro trekker had taught me: 'Take a mouthful of water. Don't swallow. Swirl it in your mouth and keep walking. This does two things—it forces you to breathe deep and breathe from your nose and not your mouth, which conserves energy. Secondly, it keeps your mouth and throat moist as the water slowly slides down your throat.' I tried this and it worked wonders.

My surroundings were even calmer in the second half of the trek. Through my body's resistance, the aches and pains, and the knee trouble, I kept going. The incessant movement was meditative and calming, allowing for deep reflection.

I had no active thoughts running in my mind. I allowed the silence of the mountains to fill my senses. For a long time, all I could hear was my own breathing, which felt as though it connected with the life all around me—of the trees, the mountains, the air, the sun, and the clouds.

I walked for a long time with the companionable silence of the hills. This calm was difficult to find and impossible to recreate. I savoured every moment of it. In this quiet space, my knee felt better, and I was infused with fresh energy to continue the rest of the way.

My meditation continued almost till I reached the Tiger's Nest. Closer to the monastery, I heard the loud gush of a waterfall. It was like a breath of fresh air; nature's symbolic collective sigh for the visitors that made it to the hilltop. Here, I heard a commotion by a group that was clicking selfies in front of the waterfall. My meditative stillness took on a joyful mood and I joined the group to click photos.

I proceeded up a steep flight of stairs into the monastery building. The interiors were raw with fading religion-themed paintings, altars in every room, statues, and paintings of Padmasambhava, and a meditation hall.

I sat in silence at the main prayer hall and tried to feel into the meditative energy that elevated Padmasambhava at this very spot. Millions trek their way up here each year in search of that energy. The hall was still but I could not sense much apart from my own beating heart. Was the point of this trek the journey rather than the destination? Perhaps it was, as is the case with most journeys.

I was relieved to be sitting cross-legged on the cool, red oxide floor, not moving, and waiting for my heart rate to stabilise. I embraced the silence, and I appreciated the opportunity to spend extended periods of time by myself without interruption.

This was a result of many years of practice in small and big ways. It started with spending hours on my own, then days, and then deeper bursts of introspection in silence. I could appreciate all that nature had to offer around me simply because I was not crumbling at the thought of being alone.

I reflected on how far I had come since my first solo trek in Switzerland. It lasted only a few hours, but it cracked open my unpreparedness for seeing what was within me. This time, years later in Bhutan, I was calmer, quieter, and more accepting of my journey and all the beauty and the flaws within me. This deserved a self-congratulatory pat.

This trek was an elevating experience in that my mind stayed with me at the moment for the entire eight-hour day. I breathed in the silence, I took in the air, I soaked in the sunshine, and I did not have to rein in my mind with too much effort. I was present and I was alive to each moment.

Being able to walk in the forest was the biggest gift. And at the end of it, to reach a Buddhist monastery was the cherry on this cake. Closing my eyes, I tried to sense any energy that might be different from what I felt on the trek up. I could feel more of the forest within the monastery; the forest was enveloping the monastery. It was the temple of nature, the temple in nature.

The more time I spent in Bhutan the more I experienced this oneness with nature. The elements were not separate from human emotions. Nature made her way into every part of Bhutanese culture, owning it and adapting to everything in a seamless way whether it was dress, food, or desires.

This understanding of the oneness in Bhutan was more powerful than what I would see on the streets in the days to come. Carrying this rich insight about the beautiful mountain country, I started the descent.

The walk back was even more difficult. My knee had given up half an hour into the descent. It was paining, excruciatingly so, preventing me from bending it or putting any weight on it, both of which I needed to do in order to keep moving.

At one point, I wondered if I need to call for help to be airlifted. I did not want to cause a fuss when I still had some energy left. So, I pushed through. I willed my mind to keep going, inspired by the beautiful views all around. People stopped by my side to give me company. I asked them to keep walking and told them that I would be right behind.

Budha came by my side and refused to leave. He gave me space, not asking me every few minutes how I felt. We walked slowly, resting at every switchback. The pain had numbed me to the extent that I lost track of time. It was getting dark, and I knew that it wasn't safe to be here in the dark. I pushed through by putting in all my might. Budha offered to carry me on his back. I refused.

We spoke to pass the time. He told me about his family and future plans. He wasn't ambitious. He preferred a balanced and stable life that included the material and spiritual. He wanted to lead a comfortable life but wouldn't compromise his values or integrity to chase money.

'There's more money to be made outside, but in another country you will always be a second-class citizen,' he said.

We walked in the twilight for what seemed like a long time. He finally said, 'The last ten minutes.' My body responded to those magical words with new energy. I walked down faster and was able to cover the last mile. When I reached the van that would take me back to my cottage, I could sigh in relief.

The trek to Tiger's Nest was a meditation—in nature, through pain, and in company. In a sense, I had experienced Padmasambhava's energy in the calming environment on the way to the monastery as well as on my way back. My physical pain was symbolic of the spiritual need to transcend the body and mind to reach a place of peace. This may have been the reason that the pain showed up to this extent only on this trek, never before or after.

That night, I tasted ara, the fermented rice drink, which was extremely strong and pungent, tasting like bitter Homoeopathic medicine, undiluted and with a dash of chili. I felt my muscles relax but didn't necessarily feel tipsy.

Spice is integral to Bhutanese food, which has mixed elements of Chinese, Tibetan, and Indian flavours. I ate a lot of red rice and vegetable stew, and even tried the local Ena Datshi, a dish made of chili, yak cheese, onion, and tomatoes. I never could acquire a taste for it in such a short span of time. I tried biting into yak cheese but spat it out instantly. It tasted like leather.

Over the course of a week, I saw more of the delightfully culture-rich country—be it food or dance, which is elegantly slow and repetitive. But the one experience that is still etched in my memory is the archery tournament. I attended one local event, which was a festive affair with buntings strung atop the large ground, and drumbeats to celebrate a bull's eye.

Archery is Bhutan's national sport, one that is taken extremely seriously. I asked Budha to explain the game's rules and he obliged. 'There are thirteen archers in each team. Everyone takes turns shooting at the target twice. The team that gets twenty-five points first is the winner.' Simple enough, I thought.

I noticed at one point that the men from one team were standing in a line and hooting and shouting. 'This is to distract the other team's archer when he's shooting,' laughed Budha. It was all fun and frolic.

I also learned that it was a cultural event as much as it was a sporting event. The aim was to gain twenty-five points, but that exercise would be dragged on for hours so that the festivities continued for the most part of the day.

When an archer hit the bull's eye, his team stood in a line and performed a synchronised dance number accompanied by drumbeats. There was never a dull moment on the field. I also heard that it was acceptable for the archers to consume alcohol before the tournament to calm their nerves.

Also, a day before important tournaments, they are to stay in a barn in the woods or someplace far away from their wives and family to avoid distraction. There are women archers, too. 'But like women's cricket in India, it is only picking up pace recently,' said Budha.

At one point there was silence on the ground as an archer was intently focusing on his aim. Budha walked up beside me and whispered: 'See that man in the shiny yellow scarf? He is the prince. He's here with his cousins for the tournament.'

I looked in the direction where Budha pointed. It was obvious that the man in question was different. The men around him stood with respectful distance and reverence.

The prince wore sunglasses and looked dignified even as he cheered his teammates on the field. He was neither too enthusiastic nor too cold.

The day dragged on, and then all too suddenly there was a melee and people were walking all over the field across the line to the target. The tournament was over. 'Wait, who won?' I asked no one in particular. I didn't get an answer. I guess it didn't matter.

The competition was important for that moment. When it was over, the day's events were forgotten and everyone moved on to the next event. So did I as I got into the taxi that drove me to a restaurant for a rice and soup lunch.

In the days that followed, I visited Bhutan's spiritual centres in chortens and dzongs (other names for monasteries). I experienced how spiritual life was embedded in Bhutanese culture. I saw too many stress-free, smiling faces living up to the country's Gross National Happiness (GNH), not Gross National Product, like in the West.

This GNH is measured through good governance, natural environment, sustainable growth, and cultural values. The Bhutanese people fed off nature. The rivers danced in happiness. The trees were free in their rootedness. The air was cool and fresh. The devout visited chortens and spun prayer wheels to carry their wishes to the universe.

This was a country with hope, but that hope didn't come in the way of their happiness. People were happy, regardless. This is a great spiritual culture that the world can benefit from. They were not out to prove a point or show anyone anything. They simply lived in peace and harmony with their mountains and rivers.

In return, nature rewarded them with great levels of peace and inner knowing. I guess it makes them the wealthiest people on earth.

22

Soaking in the Freezing Winter's Warm Glow of Lake Superior

I cupped the mug of hot tea with both hands and could feel its warmth making its way up my arms and the rest of my body. I was wearing six layers of warm clothes and still shivered at the sheets of white snow I saw outside the large glass windows of a café in Duluth, the charming Minnesota town on the northernmost edge of the United States.

Appreciating my growing love of photography, my friend Sarah, while gifting me the celebrated Brazilian photographer Sebastião Salgado's famous book *Genesis*, told me at length about Duluth. It is only a three-hour drive from Minneapolis, an easy weekend getaway, she said.

Duluth grows into every season with so much passion that the town embraces change and lets it all go when it is time to move on, she said of the town she clearly had grown to love. Not accustomed to the heavy winters of North America or anywhere for that matter, I was sceptical of how I would manage the snow-filled Duluth that would be a few degrees colder than Minneapolis.

'That is the beauty of it,' said Sarah, further tickling my already aroused curiosity.

I may have decided to visit this North American border town out of my implicit trust in Sarah's recommendations, but it was what she said about the town's special ability to embrace the seasons without fuss that had me interested. There must be something special about it, so I wanted to go there and experience it for myself.

I met Madison, my coworker's daughter, who was a college student and ice hockey player at the time. Madison made the time to guide me on short hikes to the most beautiful landscapes during my weekend in Duluth.

'Why did you decide to come to Duluth, of all places?' she asked.

'There's something beautiful to see in every part of the world. My dream is to cover every inch of it,' I told her, truthfully. 'Plus, there's Lake Superior,' I added.

Duluth was a convenient access point to experience Lake Superior, one of the five Great Lakes of North America and the world's largest freshwater lake by surface area.

As we drove outside Duluth to a hiking spot, I noticed that Madison wore only two layers of clothing while I was bundled in six layers, all tucked inside a heavy snow jacket.

Dressing for extreme winter was new to me. Think minus 24 degrees Celsius, in which the inside of a refrigerator was warmer than the streets. The threat of frostbite was real.

Gloves were a must, and so were thermals. Dressing took time and patience with all those layers of woollies. For someone from a warmer climate, and not used to layered clothing, it was a struggle to remember to wear all the pieces of clothing, and then hold on to them during the day. Gloves, woollen cap, scarf, earmuffs, the list was long. It wasn't uncommon to find a single glove abandoned on the road or a scarf casually hanging from a street-side railing, forgotten by its owner.

'Aren't you cold?' I asked her.

'No. I'm used to this. When I am indoors, I try to dress light. When stepping out for more than five minutes, of course, I need a heavy jacket, which I am carrying,' she pointed to the backseat where lay her snow jacket.

Driving in Duluth was comfortable and easy. Along the way, we stopped at strategic spots from where I saw Lake Superior in its half-frozen glory. Large blocks of ice wobbled on the lakebed. The lake shore was a giant carpet of fluffy white. This perfect winter landscape of sparkling white snow, soft sun, misty clouds, and tall trees was made more perfect by snow-covered mountains in the hazy distance.

Madison then showed me the lighthouse from the top of another mountain. We walked in the snow, touched the cold water of Lake Superior, and clicked photos. Then we went on another hike thirty minutes outside Duluth. It was shut for the winter. A signboard clearly asked visitors to keep out as the stairs were slippery from the snow, but Madison didn't care. She climbed over the wooden gate and asked me to do the same. I hesitated but followed her, not missing the adventure.

We walked down a long flight of wooden steps to another viewpoint of the lighthouse, which on its own was not impressive, but it stood tall and imposing over the landscape of water, cliffs, mountains, trees, and snow everywhere.

I imagined that Duluth might be very different in the summer. 'Duluth does justice to all four seasons. The summers are hot. Winters are cold. Spring is colourful. And autumn is bare. It is constantly changing through the year, and I love it for its ability to be every season completely,' she said.

Now in peak winter in early January, it was uncomfortable to stay outdoors for over thirty minutes. The cold was punishingly severe. So, we would run back into the car and turn on the heater.

That afternoon, Madison took me to watch an ice hockey game at the convention centre. The stadium was large, with a seating capacity of over 8,500. For a small town, it was incredibly huge. A local game was on between two school-level teams.

'Ice hockey is such a big part of North American culture. All parents want their child to be a star professional ice hockey player,' Madison said, adding, 'I have always wanted to be a professional player, too.'

'Are you good at the sport?' I asked her, putting her in a spot.

'I'm good,' she smiled shyly. 'Good players earn scholarships, travel for tournaments, and are passionately invested in the sport.' I witnessed that passion at play, with parents and coaches shouting and screaming out names and pushing players to run faster, move quicker and think smarter.

'How do children manage the pressure?' I asked her.

'It's all we see and know while growing up. We don't know any other way to be. Also, there's not a lot we can do here, it's so cold for most of the year. We can't get out much unless we live half the year somewhere else. Only the wealthy can do that. The rest of us get into ice hockey and focus on it,' she explained.

Roars of cheers and hoots echoed through the mostly empty stadium.

After Madison and I split for the day with a plan to meet the next morning for another short hike outside Duluth, I went to Amazing Grace café and watched a band comprising fifty- to seventy-year-old men play peppy country music.

I ordered a pot of tea and looked out the window to mostly empty snow-covered streets. If I saw someone walking the streets, it was only to get into or out of a car.

Cars were also few and far between—only one car drove by every 30–40 seconds.

I walked to the lakeshore to a part of Duluth where Lake Superior was completely frozen. The lake was so still that its unmoving whiteness was eerie. A part of an abandoned wooden ship stuck outside the ice. I wondered if this wooden block belonged to the SS Edmund Fitzgerald shipwreck of 1975, and floated closer to the shore, now sticking out of the water like an art installation. The stillness of the water before me made it difficult to imagine that the lake could ever be so volatile that her waves reached as high as 40 feet. In bad weather, the lake has been so rambunctious that she devoured some 6,000 ships on stormy days and nights.

Lake Superior is fed by 200 rivers and has a shoreline of over 4,300 km, some of it cutting through Canada. By the standards of the Earth's other marvellous natural wonders, Lake Superior is only 10,000 years young, formed when the glaciers retreated so many years ago. By comparison, the other largest freshwater lake, Baikal in Russia, is dated 25 million years old.

Standing in front of the frozen lake, I could not help but feel a sense of wonder. There was a mix of fear, too, because this lake did not reveal herself to me completely. Beneath her frozen layers were many hidden stories and energies that were waiting to burst forth.

Yet, in the company of her silence, a sense of tranquillity and awe washed over me. The vast expanse of water stretching out before me seemed to go on forever. The lake was both powerful and majestic. All her qualities were palpable.

In the company of the lake, I felt connected to something much greater than myself, something ancient and eternal. Reflecting on my past, I thought about the journey that had brought me to this edge of the earth. Growing up in a busy city, I was accustomed to restlessness, an anxiety that had become a part of my nature. I had even accepted it as a prerequisite for survival.

But a gut instinct pulled me towards a desire to explore other ways of living. I was drawn to go physically in search of these varied ways of thinking and being. The best way to do this was to explore the many wonders that this planet has to offer. Wandering on Mother Earth, I was discovering parts of myself that were hidden in the dark for a long time. I converted my yearning for exploration into itineraries. And off I went—to popular places and to barely known corners with only my gut feeling leading me there.

The more I saw this beautiful planet, the more I wanted to see. My dreams of exploration were fuelled by the belief that I would find my pot of gold at the end of the rainbow. My passion for discovery grew hotter and bolder. Standing before Lake Superior, I wondered where I might be along the rainbow.

The gentle ripples created by the snow-covered water brought me back to the present. In that moment, I felt content. All the challenges and uncertainties of life seemed to matter less. I felt an overwhelming gratitude for the opportunity to experience such natural beauty and to be alive right here, right now. As I breathed in the fresh air and felt the cold breeze on my skin, I encountered within me a renewed sense of energy and purpose.

That moment was a synchronous meeting of the past, present, and future. While I considered how my past brought me here, I was also deeply aware of life's endless possibilities. I felt excited and hopeful for what lay ahead. The lake stood as the proof I needed to see that whatever the challenges or obstacles, I will somehow find the strength and resilience to overcome them. As long as I remained open to the wonders of the world around me, I was confident that I would find my way home.

Lake Superior was showing me that life was a journey of discovery, a never-ending quest to explore the mysteries of the world and our place in it. The destination might be unknown, but the journey itself is what truly mattered.

As I gazed out at the vast expanse of water and the icy shape it had taken, I could only bow in gratitude for its beauty and for the opportunity to be a part of this moment. I felt that a part of me was healing right there in that silence.

Water has always held a special place in my heart, and its healing power has been a constant source of strength throughout my life. I have feared water when learning to swim but also embraced its fluidity, marvelled at its qualities, and in my spiritual journey, been humbled by its greatness.

I came to realise that water was more than just a physical element; it was a powerful force that could transform and heal the soul. I was introduced to its soothing and restorative properties.

Whenever I felt lost, uncertain, or overwhelmed, I would turn to water, whether it was through swimming, taking a bath, or simply sitting by a stream or a waterfall, or even drinking water mindfully. The sound of water flowing and the sensation of being enveloped by its coolness and purity enhanced my peace and clarity in a way that I could not find with any other element.

Water also appeared in my dreams, often as a symbol of transformation and renewal. At the most important transitions in my life, I have dreamt of huge waves washing ashore where I stood. I was terrified in the dreams but only later understood that the water was showing me a mirror to my emotions. Water showed me how deeply I felt, and how much something or someone mattered to me.

In many dreams, I would find myself diving into the depths of a lake or an ocean, exploring the mysterious and mystical realm beneath the surface. The deeper I dove into her depths, the water would wash away my fears and doubts, revealing hidden truths and guiding me towards a better understanding of myself and the world around me.

Over time, water became an integral part of my spiritual practice, playing a central role in my growth and evolution. I began to understand water as a powerful metaphor for the soul's journey, a reminder that even in the darkest of times, there is always a source of light and hope that can guide us towards a brighter future.

Through my deep relationship with water, I have come to realise that healing and transformation are possible, no matter how lost or broken we may feel. Water teaches us that we are never truly alone, and that there is always a force greater than ourselves to support and guide us along our journey.

Travelling alone to remote places can be life-changing. This was one such moment when I understood the full depth and importance of solo travel. I was connecting with one of the most important elements of nature here. It was directly related to my spiritual growth. Such journeys have opened new life perspectives. I have come to appreciate the beauty and diversity of our earth in ways I never thought possible.

When travelling alone, I can be alone but not necessarily lonely. I can reflect without interruption. I can heal without doubt and confusion. I can contemplate the deeper questions of life by grabbing moments of stillness. I can check in on my values, priorities, and purpose. I can try to find the clarity and direction. Solo travel may not get it all perfect the first time around, but it is an art and a practice that has made me get better at it over the years.

I have stumbled upon insights and found solutions when hiking in the mountains, kayaking in the river, or simply walking through a forest, being surrounded by everything that is natural. These have been the most profound experiences rather than the ones I have had sitting in a place of religious worship.

It is when out in nature that I have felt the interconnectedness of all life and developed a deep reverence for the natural beauty and power of this world. I may go to the mountains or a remote place to see a lake, but if I do not carry the intent to heal, all this travel is only but a movement from one place to another. When the mind, heart, and intentions connect with the environment around us, magic is created. It can be a transformative spiritual experience. But getting the mind, heart, and our intentions ready for such transformation is also a matter of timing and luck.

When several of these factors come together, then nature can be the most healing energy. She can heal us by revealing to us her deeper truths and mysteries of the universe. Whether it is through meditation, prayer, or simply being present in the moment, we can tap into a source of wisdom and guidance that is beyond our individual selves to find peace and purpose that transcends our everyday worries.

I found such clarity in this moment standing before Lake Superior. I closed my eyes for a long time in gratitude for this moment and for all the moments before that were necessary to bring me here.

The ice-cold winds made it uncomfortable to stand there any longer. I walked towards a bridge where the water wasn't frozen, urging my mind and attention to return to more mundane things.

Along the way, I saw hotels on the shore with private balconies for each room facing the lake. I imagined the lake shores buzzing with activity in the summer. There were a handful of people by the bridge, clicking photos of the lake and the Duluth cityscape. Ducks paddled about, the only sign of life I saw on the cold lake.

On the next day, too, I followed the same routine. I went on a hike with Madison to experience a different landscape from a mountaintop. We then went to a pub to watch what she said was an important ice hockey league match. Madison explained the rules and spoke about the teams and why they mattered.

We spoke for a long time after which Madison was more engrossed in the game as it came to a crucial point. I let Madison watch the rest of the game in peace while I returned to Amazing Grace café. On that afternoon, no band played. It was still crowded but I got a seat by the window. Sitting there, I felt like a local in Duluth, even if only for the weekend.

This is the beauty of small towns with their minimum distractions, and limited choice in shopping, entertainment, or even social life.

In two days, I had experienced a slice of North American town life with its extreme cold and sporting passion. I was ready to return to a warmer place.

I had booked a shared ride from Duluth to St Paul International Airport. On the ride, I met seven North Americans, all of whom had never set foot outside the Minnesota state. They asked me many questions and were eager to share bits from their life.

The van driver told me that he had never seen a solo Indian woman traveller in the US Midwest region, and that, too, in the dead of winter when vacationers visited only for group winter sports like snowmobiling or skiing.

We headed into the town centre on the way out to the freeway and he proudly showed off Duluth from the top of the sloping road. As we drove down the very steep road, the views of the lake and the buildings were spectacular, offering a bird's eye view of the town that I had seen up close over two days.

When the conversations slowed, I wore headphones and listened to soulful instrumental music while taking in the white scenery all around. We had driven for about forty-five minutes on near-perfect straight roads when it started to snow. It was the first time I was driving in the snow. It was magical, with snowflakes hitting the windscreen and turning into spots of water.

When we took a break, the group of Americans had more questions for me.

'Do Indian women come out of the house?'

'What kind of food do you eat?'

'Is Indian your national language?'

'Are all Indian languages similar? Do they use characters or letters?'

'Do you have currency in India? What money do you use?'

I answered their questions and then pulled out a Rs 500 note from my wallet to show them. One of the women pointed to Gandhi's image on the note and asked me who he was. She had never heard of Mahatma Gandhi.

A woman asked me if I had babies. I said no. She said she had one baby. 'I miss her very much, and I'm so excited to see her when I get home,' she said.

After a brief pause, she said: 'Do you want to see a photograph?' I nodded. She pulled her iPhone out and handed it to me. On the screen was the photograph of a white chihuahua with black spots, staring at me with a deadpan expression.

The woman looked at me eagerly, hoping for a reaction. 'That's . . . sweet,' was all I could manage. I smiled awkwardly and handed back her phone.

She took the phone back and started to talk about her baby. 'I take my baby along on vacations. But some people don't like dogs in their houses. I had such a rough time on the last vacation because the hosts were unhappy with my baby shedding hair on their furniture,' she said.

The chatter subsided again, and the passengers looked out the window, napped, snacked, or simply stared at the road ahead. This was a part of America that was so self-absorbed that it didn't wander out too far in search of the unfamiliar or the new.

In these few hours on the ride, I happened to be that stranger that came into town with stories and a life perspective that was different from theirs. This part of the world is not limited in its access to the rest of the earth, but most people here seem to not quite know what to do with that access.

Content with the zoomed-in focus on their immediate problems and worries, the people that I met in Duluth played out their life stories completely in the moment. On the larger karmic stage, they were but actors unaware of their roles but were playing them anyway.

I reached the airport and said a warm goodbye to everyone before dragging my bags from the cold into the air-conditioned warmth of the airport terminal.

The airport terminal—that meeting place of beginnings and endings, the place where the past meets the future, and the place from where dreams and promises take off and land.

Most people cannot wait to get out of an airport terminal. Its cold food served in impersonal paper and plastic cutlery, uncomfortable seating, stale air, and messy toilets are enough to chase passengers further away to new destinations. But I love to spend time here as this transitional ground carries the least amount of baggage and judgment. I check in here for a flight, but I also check in to my emotions, shedding the excess weight carried from the place and the people that I am leaving behind while giving a carte blanche to my heart to fully embrace the place that I am headed to.

An airport terminal is that brief pause, the sigh of relief between adventures, the goodbye before the hello, and it is the temple teaching us that an ending always means a new beginning.

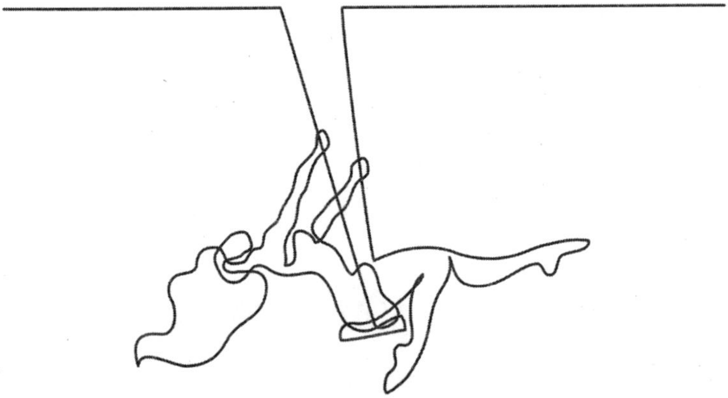

I TRANSCEND

These are places where the veil between dimensions is thin. Setting foot on this land, touching the rocks here, letting the sand from these places slip through my fingers, and breathing this air all transported me to a spiritual plane that only many years of meditation in my temple may have achieved.

These are gateways to heaven on earth.

23

Wading with Sea Turtles in Hikkaduwa

I slid my feet into leathery fins and swam behind the instructor into the warmth of the Indian Ocean. The water was warmer than I had expected. I bit hard into the snorkelling gear and breathed deep through my mouth, the air flowing through the angled plastic pipe.

The instructor led me by hand as I looked underwater, marvelling at the diversity of sea life. This was only meters away from the shore. I wondered what mysteries the waters hid deep inside the ocean. I was seeing colours that I had never seen in my life. I saw at least five shades of red, blue, bright orange, purple, magenta, black and white. While all my attention was underwater, the instructor tugged at my hand leading me farther into the deep waters. Not used to breathing from my mouth for so long, I felt tired. I was about to signal for a break when I spotted the sea turtle. My world froze in time.

This moment was my pause in meditation—that emptiness beyond time and space. There, underwater and swimming inches away from a sea turtle, everything else ceased to exist for me. It didn't matter that the goggles were too tight or that I didn't like spitting on them to clean them. It didn't matter that my plastic fins were too heavy, and it took a bit of practice to swim with them. It didn't matter that the tourist motorboats zipping across only inches away from me were too loud and their diesel fumes, too polluting. Nothing mattered.

I moved my legs and arms just enough to stay at that spot as close to the sea turtle for as long as I could. The turtle barely moved her limbs, gently swaying in the water. I didn't hear anything else, and I couldn't see anything else. It was the kind of powerful moment that reached into the depths of my heart to connect with the one emotion that mattered most, gratitude.

As the turtle gently moved her arms, it looked like an angel waving her wand of love and magic all around. I had read about turtles and what wondrous creatures they were—their longevity, survival instinct, and intelligence. But all that was textbook information.

Swimming in the ocean with the sea turtle was a transformative experience in which, through her majesty and grace, I had access to the beauty and mystery of the natural world. I floated in the warm waters and felt weightless and free. The gentle swaying of the water was soothing . . . it was dancing with me. And I had the sea turtle for company.

My mind had gone quiet, but my heart was full of reverence for this complete experience. The turtle was showing me how to slow down, and what beauty there is in simply allowing life to go at its own pace without forcing anything.

I also felt one with the universe at that moment. The turtle, the water, and me—we were all interconnected as a part of the same ecosystem. I had never felt more accepted than in that moment. It reminded me of my place in the world. I am a part of it, I don't own anything, yet I have a right to be here. Swimming with the sea turtle was a call to develop a deeper connection to the earth and reverence for all life around me.

There, I was experiencing this animal's poise and beauty, and feeling into the turtle's power of resilience. It was only fitting that of all places in the world, I got to experience the turtle in Sri Lanka, whose people had to tap into their own reserves of resilience in recent years.

I was visiting Hikkaduwa, a four-km coastal stretch in the south-western tip of Sri Lanka, on a week-long vacation. About 120 km from Sri Lanka's capital city Colombo, the three-hour drive along the coastline to Hikkaduwa was busy with incessant traffic.

I chose Hikkaduwa over Colombo's history and Nuwaya Eliya's tea estates for its reputation as a hip vacation spot that was casting off its lethargic past to embrace an optimistic future. Hikkaduwa was aspiring to be known as a party hotspot with its beaches, music, and cheery vibe.

Besides the slanting coconut trees, warm hospitality, unpredictable weather, tasty food, heritage train stations, narrow winding roads, Hikkaduwa tucked away many other surprises in the folds of her heart making a visit to this town a traveller's delight.

This town displayed few visible signs of the country's deep crises, working hard to shed its baggage from the twenty-six-year Civil War and the 2004 tsunami. But upon scratching the surface only lightly, its struggles and darkness from the not-yet-distant past emerged in full view.

I was visiting the country eight years after the tsunami hit but I could still see in the Hikkaduwans' eyes a mix of terror, grief, and loss at any mention of the disaster. The tsunami punctuated the survivor's lives in a clear before-and-after that forever transformed their spirituality and world view.

What also made the change more difficult for Hikkaduwa specifically was the pressure of a vacation spot to be a happy place. Tourists feed off happy energy. So, to run its beach shacks, restaurants, and dive centres successfully, it needed to give off that cheerful vibe. On the surface, the locals had come a long way, rebuilding the place brick by brick. But it was their emotions that would take time to heal.

I got the strongest insight into Hikkaduwans and Sri Lanka from my snorkelling instructor, Chaminda Leelan, who I will always remember as the kind-hearted soul that gifted me the invaluable experience of swimming alongside a sea turtle. Chaminda ran the Poseidon Dive Centre. Well into midlife, Chaminda carried an invisible weight on him that was only apparent on deeper observation.

He was the big boss at the centre and made the major decisions, instructed his crew on who would lead the day's diving lessons, made tourists feel comfortable and safe, and was constantly busy running the place. But when he snatched moments alone between the busyness, he would stare unfazed and with dispassion at the horizon, where water met sky. This was not just a fixed gaze or a meditation. He travelled great distances in his mind before returning to the present.

I went to the dive centre a few times during the week and would chat him up. He was initially resistant to sharing his story. At the first mention of the tsunami, his eyes grew dark and he clammed up. I stopped asking questions that I thought might make him uncomfortable. When talking about food, music, the best party spots in town, he seemed uninterested but shared information. I thought I saw his eyes flicker with just a bit of hope when he spoke about a fish barbecue at his centre that evening.

A couple of days later, we swam farther away from the shore to see a shoal of fish that Chaminda said was rare and vibrantly colourful. We saw the red-coloured fish and also spotted two turtles on the way back. Resting on the beach, Chaminda spoke from his heart. He said that his father had started this diving centre years ago, which the tsunami turned into rubble. He lost everything that was dear to him.

'I was not near the shore when it happened, but I ran here as fast as I could when I heard. I have not seen devastation like that ever before, and I hope I never see that again. I jumped into the water immediately with a few other survivors to try and save people. But it was not enough,' he said.

Chaminda acknowledged that he needed time and distance to heal the scars on both his life and spirit. I thought of the turtle as a symbol of strength and resilience, continuing to give hope to the survivors. 'Being so close to nature must help the healing process, no?' I asked.

'You always have nature for company, but what do you do when the very thing that you rely on turns on you? Who will you blame in this situation?' he said, voicing his feelings of betrayal and even anger at the water.

He sighed after a long silence and said, 'But go on, we must.'

We watched as dark clouds gathered indicating that it would rain. All the divers and tourists were asked to move back under the shelter. Chaminda stared at the dark-grey water and the roaring waves crashing into the shore.

He ran towards the water and dove in to swim a few laps. This was his ongoing effort to manage his relationship with water. Water had changed his life forever, but he had to keep his relationship alive. It was his source of livelihood. It was also his home. This carrying on, really, is the resilience of the human spirit.

That evening, I went for a walk inland, away from the beach. I lost my way on the winding roads and spotted a signboard for a Buddhist temple. I followed the narrow road and passed a stream. I saw monks in ochre robes stepping out of the temple.

I walked up the flight of stairs to an opening, which housed a pagoda and many small structures with idols of the Buddha avatars. It was empty, peaceful, and quiet inside. I met a monk, Rajendra, who had serene eyes and a gentle manner about him. He showed me around the temple while explaining its history. The 300-year-old temple in Baddegama neighbourhood of Hikkaduwa was a huge draw for the locals to offer prayers and sit in meditation.

A large bodhi tree stretched out its branches over the lawns. I saw a Sinhalese couple in their twenties offering prayers under the tree. They lit incense sticks and sat on the grass to enjoy the peace and quiet. I sat next to them. The lady opened a small prayer book, from which she started chanting mantras. I whispered to the man asking if the language was Sinhalese. He nodded.

I didn't understand a word of the chants. But I sat there listening till she finished the entire prayer. The tone of the chants and the lilt in her voice were like a soothing lullaby.

I was immersed in the repetitive chants, their unfamiliar sounds and rhythms, and my heart responded with a calm joy.

The repetition created a hypnotic effect, drawing me in and allowing me to lose myself in their comforting sway. It was unlike anything I had heard before, yet I felt as though I was riding on some transformative sound waves. The rhythm shifted in a few minutes. It sounded like a louder, more persistent call to the universe to listen in. The subtle nuances of the shifting patterns took me along on the spiritual ride. I went along, happily so.

My mind and energy were tuned in to the chants. A while later my body responded, too. I was swaying to the rhythm. I experienced warm tingling in my limbs as the sounds tickled the energy channels in my body. I was opening up to the world around me.

The incense smelled stronger. I could feel it go all the way to my lungs, creating a cleansing effect on my airways. I was lost in the repetitive chants, my senses were heightened, and a welling of gratitude burst forth from my heart centre. I did not need to understand the meaning of the chants to experience their effect. My senses had transcended beyond the limits of the physical world and were connecting with something greater than what I saw and understood around me.

In my most memorable experiences in Sri Lanka, of swimming along sea turtles and being part of a chanting experience at a Buddhist temple, I could break free from the limitations of the physical world to connect with a higher state of awareness.

I became conscious of the larger web of life, the interconnectedness of all things in the universe. I credit immersive travel experiences with the ability to take us to such deeper levels of awareness.

Transcending is also about pushing my own limits and getting outside my comfort zone in my physical, mental, and emotional worlds. It is about flirting with the unknown and conquering fear. It is also about wading into uncertainty and being okay with not knowing all the answers.

When I opened my eyes at the end of the chants, I felt like a different person. I thanked the couple for this unique spiritual experience.

In the days that followed, I immersed myself even further in my understanding of Sri Lanka. I spoke to tuk-

tuk drivers, storekeepers, monks, and the locals going about their daily life. Their stories revealed that for an average Sri Lankan every day was a struggle to transcend the country's turbulent history.

In Hikkaduwa, foreign tourists are helping locals make new memories and forge new friendships to speed up the land's healing and transition. In this, the role of the visitors, the outsiders, who bring stories from their land, is as important for the locals as the locals are important for the visiting vacationers' experience of the country.

Sri Lanka's raw beauty and its centres of calm—its Buddhist temples—balance the people's internal strife. It all resonated with me. Every story that I encountered during my time in Sri Lanka contributed to my larger spiritual experience.

Sri Lanka taught me about overcoming adversity. It is truly an island of hope.

24

Myths and Legends Live on in Olkhon Island's Cliffs of Time

The conspicuous crack on the windshield was not a welcome sight when I got into the van's front passenger seat. I had seen in the movies that this was the way glass shattered from a bullet shot. I casually turned to the driver, who was cursing under his breath. He was visibly stressed about getting us, a group of travellers, to our destination.

I decided not to start a conversation with him just yet. I would wait. We had six hours on the road from Irkutsk to Olkhon Island, and much could happen in that time. I was among the first to be picked up and so got the front seat, which is my favourite for long rides. You get a good view of the road while chatting up the driver.

The driver stopped at other hotels across central Irkutsk for scheduled pick-ups. With about ten passengers in the van, we hit the highway. The van was mostly silent, barring the dull hum of the engine and the occasional conversation between passengers, who spoke in low voices at the back.

The open road and the view of dales and horse ranches along the way had done the driver a world of good. He seemed lighter in mood, his face muscles were not as tense, and his shoulders were relaxed.

I looked out, too, with nervous anticipation of what I would find at Olkhon Island. Some places are much better in our minds than they are when we finally see them. I wondered, and knew to an extent to be true, that I had worked up grand expectations of Burkhan Cape in the run-up to my month-long expedition across the length of Russia.

In my spiritual explorations, I had heard about Siberian shamanism as a powerful practice of connecting with nature. And Burkhan Cape in Olkhon Island was the presiding temple of this shamanism. 'Burkhan Cape is to Siberian shamans what Tirupati is to Hindus,' my friend Joseph told me.

He told me to not climb the rocks at this cape. 'You would never touch something sacred with your feet, would you?' he asked.

I had heard stories of deep healing at this place; people's lives had transformed once they had set foot here. The beauty of this natural healing centre, apart from its obvious physical location in the deep part of Siberia, was as much in its difficulty for the rest of the world to access it.

Making a trip here—if one truly wanted to experience the capital of Siberian shamanism—demanded commitment and honesty. Of course, many European and American backpackers with little interest or prior knowledge of shamanism visit this island, but more as clueless tourists and less as aficionados of an animistic practice.

One needed to plan a visit here, sparing many days and much determination. It was not a one-flight one-taxi ride kind of a destination. The island had evolved over the years as an off-beat economical vacation spot for discerning European and American travellers who had likely ticked off most places on the must-visit easy-to-reach list in the world.

My reasons for visiting Olkhon Island were a mix of curiosity and a spiritual draw that didn't let me doubt my decision. Cape Burkhan came up in my meditations several times in the years leading up to my Russia travel plan. It was not the main reason but a considerably strong reason that propelled me onward with an ambitious month-long itinerary.

I felt a strong emotional connection to Lake Baikal, as though I already knew her. To touch the waters of the lake from this sacred point on Olkhon Island was meant to be a transcendental experience. I went there seeking that experience.

At the same time, I was acutely aware of the possibility that I was building up the island in my mind to such an extent that I was setting it up to fail in reality.

The mystery of many places is retained by the images we build in our minds. Those images sometimes end up being far superior to the actual place. Had I set up Olkhon Island so impossibly large in my mind that it was about to fail when I saw it? I was nervous about this mismatched expectation that I was forcing on myself.

My thoughts were interrupted by the driver, who initiated a conversation.

'Where you from?' he asked, making an effort to speak in English with the few words he knew.

When I told him, he asked, 'Indians don't eat cow, yes?'

'Many Indians do eat cow meat. Many others don't,' I told him.

'Do you eat cow?' he asked.

'No,' I replied.

It was my turn to ask questions. I started with his name—Alexey—and asked about his life. He replied as best he could, and then with one hand still on the steering wheel, pulled out the phone with the other to use the translator app to ask me if I was married, had a boyfriend, or if I had children. Alexey showed me his girlfriend's photo.

I thought this was a good time to ask the question that was on my mind since morning.

'How did this happen?' I pointed to the crack on the windshield and hesitatingly folded my right hand to look like a gun with index and middle fingers pointed straight. I let out an awkward gunshot sound to complete the effect of what I was conveying.

Alexey's face hardened and he looked at me sternly but could only hold it for a few seconds before he burst out laughing.

He laughed for a full minute before saying, 'What? You thought all Russians mafia? You mad?'

Embarrassed, I shrugged.

'Nooo . . . This was stupid accident,' he said, and laughed again.

This exchange lightened the mood in the van as there were giggles all around.

As we drove along the winding two-lane highway with steep gradients, we saw farms and farm animals. Every time Alexey spotted a cow, he pointed to it and said, 'Lunch', and then emphasised, 'Russian lunch.'

I played along and said, 'Yummy. I'm hungry again.'

The landscape changed to flat and dry stretches of uneven land as far as the eye could see. The van slowed down on a bumpy mud road from where Lake Baikal was visible. We got closer and stopped near a jetty. I walked to the edge of the broad jetty to look out at the brown, dry hills jutting out of the bright blue water.

The cold, accompanied by biting winds, harshly cut through my thick jacket, finding every gap to slip in and challenge the warmth. Here was a taste of the unpredictable Siberian cold that competed with the midday sun. It looked bright and sunny, like a perfect summer day, but the cold demanded that you dip into your reserves of fortitude to get through the discomfort.

'You can never tell with Siberian cold. It has a mind of its own,' my friend Dina had told me only a few days ago when I asked her to share packing tips for my short visit to Olkhon Island.

I now understood the evasive answers to my questions about Siberian weather, which was temperamental and mysterious, like a woman's heart. Who could ever tell what tomorrow could look like?

The passengers walked about near the jetty, but only for a few minutes before returning to the comfort of warmth and company in the van. I did the same.

Shortly after, a catamaran arrived, stopping by the jetty, its flap gates sliding open with a giant thud that echoed through the hills and open space. The still air was disturbed as the vans and cars parked inside the catamaran reversed out, making much noise and releasing thick diesel fumes. The waiting vehicles on this side of the island drove into the catamaran in an orderly fashion, and we crossed the waters.

I got out of the van and braved the cold wind for an unobstructed view of the changing landscape. At the end of the short fifteen-minute ride, the vehicles were noisily piling out of the catamaran onto Olkhon Island.

We were now driving on bumpy, uneven ground, with the lake on the left. There was no paved road or directions marked for vehicles. We bounced, shook, and rattled along shallow and deep ditches that were somewhat levelled through overuse. Then the village came into view in the far distance, with its cluster of Siberian houses made of wooden slats and thatched roofs.

Khuzhir Village was the largest of five villages on Olkhon Island with a population of about 1,200. In the village, we drove along impossibly wide roads—unpaved mud roads but even stretches with loose gravel — leaving behind a large cloud of dust. The entire village had a total of ten roads, but each street was so wide that it would fit six buses lined up side by side.

With such wide roads and almost no human or vehicular traffic for most of the day—maybe one car would drive past in thirty minutes—made for an eerie calm that my city-bred mind, infused with constant noise, found uncomfortable.

Alexey dropped me off at my guesthouse as I waved goodbye to the balloon of dust left behind by the van. At the guesthouse, which was a property with five structures and a yard to cut and store firewood, I met Olga, the matronly owner and caretaker of the guesthouse.

Olga had green eyes and short hair coloured in a shade of maroon-burgundy. Dressed in collared t-shirt, boots, and jacket, she ran the household and was a strong presence for both family and guests.

Olga spoke no English and I spoke no Russian, but it didn't bother her. She would write the important matters on a sheet of paper and hand it to me. As soon as I settled down into my warm and cosy room, I went into the dining room for dinner. She handed me a piece of paper with the room rent for three days. I was in the middle of dinner, but Olga was staring at me, waiting. So, I went to my room to bring the cash.

Olga then said, 'Breakfast. Dinner,' pointing to the table with her index finger. 'Lunch. No.' I nodded.

Having exhausted all her English, Olga abruptly walked away.

Olga's family ate at the same dining hall, taking the corner table that was closest to the kitchen. The hall had five tables that could comfortably seat six each. Olga's husband, daughter, and an older woman—who could have been Olga's mother or mother-in-law or aunt—all dined together.

I had more than a generous glimpse of Russian rural life through Olga's family. I saw the elderly woman deeply engrossed in a Russian soap that played all the time, day and night, on a TV fixed above the kitchen platform. The family ran a cheese business; I would see them packaging cheese at the kitchen counter.

On school mornings, I saw Olga's daughter in her school uniform and thought that her impeccably white socks that stopped just below her knees were simply not warm enough for this harsh winter. I sat near the heater wrapped up in six layers of warm clothing while eating a heavy breakfast and wondering if her knees wouldn't go numb from this cold.

The food at Olga's was warm, delicious, and way too much for one person. She laid out a spread of salad, sandwiches, rice, fruits, and dessert. I was the only guest on the first two days and wondered if I was supposed to finish all the food.

The etiquette was different in every part of the world, and I wanted to be sure to do the right thing. I ate slowly but managed to finish everything on the plate. I would walk away most of the calories the next day anyway . . . I hoped.

On the second day, I saw more food on the table than the previous day. I wouldn't be able to finish all of this, I thought to myself, but tried anyway and failed.

On the third day, an Irish backpacker stayed at the guesthouse and we dined together. We talked about the quantity of food.

'I wondered the same thing everywhere I went,' she said, and pulled up an internet search for dining etiquette in Russia.

'Ah! This makes sense,' she mumbled while reading, and then told me, 'you're supposed to leave some food on the plate so that the host knows that you've eaten enough. If you wipe it clean, it probably means that you could have eaten more. So, they serve you more the next day.'

I could only laugh at this cultural mistranslation.

On the first evening that I arrived in Khuzhir, I walked around the village and in about thirty minutes of slow-paced walking, I had oriented myself quite well. Every house, only metres away from the lake, was a mild variation of the typical Siberian wooden house, with changes in colour, size, elevation, carved wooden awnings, and decorative nameplates.

The village was quiet for May; peak season time was July and August when the summer months brought tourists by the hordes. I read that vans offering the Russian steam bath experience would be parked along the lake, and tourists swam in its warm waters. But now, the village stood quiet and still.

The island was known for its beauty and was also a significant centre of Siberian shamanism or yellow shamanism, so called as it was practiced in parts of Mongolia and Siberia by incorporating elements of Buddhism.

Buryats, the indigenous aboriginal people who typically follow this culture revere the Oikony Noyod, or the thirteen lords of Olkhon, a group of deities said to originate on the Olkhon Island. For the Buryats, Olkhon Island was a pilgrimage, and the Shaman Rock, their sacred temple.

Excited to get my first glimpse of the Shaman Rock, I walked to the end of the village and around Nikita's Homestead, a popular circular-shaped guesthouse for western backpackers. A five-minute walk up and then down a slope of dry grass fields opened up to the vast Lake Baikal, stretching out in all her glistening beauty before me.

A faded, rusting metal board in Russian mentioned that this was Cape Burkhan, also known as Cape Shaman. The board also gave a longer description of the cape's religious significance.

That was it. Not grand announcements, and no other stately gestures of welcome.

I stood on top of a hill, overlooking the blue waters and the distinct rock about forty metres high, which was the shining jewel of Buryatian shamanism, the Shamanka rock. A gravel pathway cut through the water and curved towards this rock.

I was struck by the simplicity and lack of human intervention to protect this rock from defacing by mischief-minded visitors. The Shamanka was one of the nine most sacred places in Asia. Burkhan, a religious figure of the Altai Turkish indigenous people and the spirit master of Olkhon Island, was believed to live in a cave in this rock. And yet there were no barricades to prevent people from climbing on it. It was accessible to everyone—human and animals, and that was, perhaps, what made it so powerful. It stood there strong and confident in the knowledge that no external influence could shake its core.

I woke up the next morning to menacingly dark-grey clouds, biting harsh cold winds, and a hundred per cent chance of rain. I had signed up for a day trip to Cape Xoboi (pronounced Ho-boy) on the northern edge of the island. I expected it to be a difficult day in this weather.

Olkhon, described as woody and dry, gets scanty rain, if at all, throughout the year. It was a pleasant surprise, therefore, to catch the rain in the few days that I spent there. Despite the gloomy weather, the trip was on schedule. I was the first to be picked up, and I again chose the passenger seat. The van was a matte-grey retro beauty, the classic UAZ 452, a sturdy off-roader used by the military. This brand of vans was produced between 1965 and 1979 and are still used across Russia to cross difficult terrain. The van was nicknamed *bukhankha*, meaning loaf of bread because it looked like one.

We drove through the now-familiar Khuzhir village, picking up other travellers, including a Russian man, two Russian women, and three Polish men, who were travelling together. One of the Poles was an enthusiastic man in his late fifties who became the self-appointed group leader and ensured that everyone knew everyone else. Zbigniew shook my hand, learnt to pronounce my name correctly, and infused the dull-grey van with sunshine and cheer.

Everyone in the van spoke Russian, except me. Sitting in the front seat and not knowing the language, it would have been easy for me to be isolated from the group. But Zbigniew made every effort to include me in the group's banter. At the end of every conversation, he would translate it all to English for my benefit. When he struggled with some English words, he would ask his friends for help and would ensure that they did a good job.

Zbigniew was a chiropractor and serious hobbyist photographer. He travelled with two men in their thirties, who were former colleagues-turned-friends. The three men were on the day trip to Cape Xoboi at the end of the elliptical-shaped island but planned to get off at a village near there and trek their way back through the forest, camping in the wild and experiencing the island, slow and up close.

The ride was bumpy, to put it mildly. The quiet but efficient driver, Dmitry, navigated the van, steering it to any part of the ground that looked most flat. While at this, he didn't compromise on the speed. I held on tightly, feeling my insides getting a good rattle and churn. At the first stop, we caught a picturesque view of the lake.

Standing at the edge of the cliff, I could see the almost-black clouds hovering just above the water, which reflected a spine-chilling black colour. This scenery was cold in every way, just one of the avatars of Baikal. On the horizon, sunlight beamed on a range of brown mountains all lined up in perfect harmony, same height and width.

Everyone in the group dispersed into different parts of the mountain to find privacy and click photos from what each thought was the vantage point. In ten minutes, we gathered to click group photos.

Andrzej, a doctor in Poland, constantly made up stories about myths and legends associated with Lake Baikal. He talked with deep conviction in his stories about monsters, dinosaurs, lions, and tigers.

On this first attempt at selling me these stories, I took the bait. When I realised a few seconds later, it was too late, and I had become the butt of jokes. All kinds of absurd and outlandish stories about the myths and legends of Baikal were narrated through the day, often catching me off-guard and putting my vulnerability up for display. I played along. After all, here were strangers who laughed with you, not at you.

We drove for six hours during the day, stopping at ten viewpoints along the way, between rough rides and hiking up slopes and climbing mountaintops to experience Lake Baikal from every angle possible. Every single time I stood at the edge of the cliff and looked at the expanse of Baikal, I was filled with incredulity for the wonder that is nature. The mind breached the wall of thoughts and entered the zone of unthinking alertness, the cyclical space with no beginning or end, the stillness where everything was forgotten and forgiven, the emotion of oneness with the universe, the rhythm of throbbing to one heartbeat, humming the same tune, an all-knowing, all-pervading universality.

This was a powerful meditation that flowed into itself, from and to nothing, and self-contained like Baikal herself. Here, on the edge of the cliff, I didn't need to make an effort to get to this state of pulsating aliveness.

It is this moment that seekers crave and travellers chase. Baikal had made this possible for me, grabbing me in her bosom and hugging me tight, making me listen to her heartbeat, the pulse of the universe.

On these cliffs of time, the veils between worlds thinned, opening a gateway to another world of emotions and spirit. From here, there was more to know, learn, and experience.

The now-familiar spaciousness and beauty of Baikal, and the alive state of mind carried into the laughter with the group, the short treks, and the conversations.

Our last stop was a forty-minute round trip hike up a hillock, where a pole was decorated with colourful prayer flags. Coins as offerings lay strewn on the ground around this pole. The locals believed that some offering is a must when visiting such sacred places. The value of the offering doesn't matter as long as you leave behind something that is yours. It is a small sacrifice in the hope of prayers answered.

By now, a heavy drizzle had started, so we rushed down the hill to the van where Dmitry had laid out lunch on a wooden table next to the trees. We welcomed the hot tea, bread, and Omul fish soup, a delicacy available only in this part of Siberia. Omul, a naturally salty fish, is found only in Lake Baikal, and is a treat for fish eaters.

We saw chickens and ducks walking about near where we sat. Then we saw a fox walk past. The fox was looking for food, so Dmitry threw a slice of bread in the air and the fox caught it. It stared at each one of us with intelligent eyes, as though assessing us, before walking away in a gracefully slow manner.

The drive back was tiring again with the bumpy ride, and after dropping off Zbigniew and his two Polish friends at a remote two-house village on the lakeshore, Dmitry and the superhero van brought the rest of us home safe.

* * *

On my last day at the island, I had a free day to spend with the lake. I walked down to the Shamanka and sat with the stillness for a long time. I washed my hands in the icy cold waters, wrote, daydreamed, meditated, and sat in the quiet but powerful company of Baikal. There was no chatter within or outside to take me away from that inner quietude. The winds howled a bit and birds whistled, often flying too close to me for comfort.

Baikal was a mystery that she wasn't going to reveal to everyone easily. She was a prayer waiting to be answered, and a friend with many secrets in her pockets. She could be compassionate and fierce, stable, and delicate. But the emotion that stayed with me was that of a mother who looked out for her brood.

It was difficult to walk away from Baikal at the end of the day. My heart refused to let go, so my mind reasoned. I pulled out a coin and offered it to the lake with a promise to see her again. The world runs on the promise of another day. It is said: 'A promise is a cloud. Fulfilment is rain.'

As though to signal that my promise was heard, it rained as I slowly walked back to Olga's house. I didn't run for cover or wait for the rain to stop. I continued walking in the promise of another time, another day.

25

Tearing through a Tornado to Trek the Grand Canyon

A tornado warning had forced the pilot on my Miami-Phoenix flight to make an emergency landing midway in Houston. I looked out the window and saw a long line of diverted flights waiting for instructions.

It was 11 p.m. and all I needed was a comfortable bed to sleep off the fatigue from a long day at the conference in Miami. Instead, I was served this unexpected excursion of diverted flights and long waits on the runway.

We were not alone on the runway, which was comforting. I rested my forehead against the window and tried to sleep but I was woken up with an announcement that we were all to deboard. A collective groan filled the cabin's stale air.

I stayed awake, waiting to get off the plane. After what seemed like almost an hour, a steward announced that we were to stay seated and await further instructions. I heard a male co-passenger's voice, 'The terminal is so crowded that they can't have any more of us get off the planes and go in there.'

I catnapped between assurances and further announcements that there would be more updates. From the window, the pitch-black night sky looked dark and dangerous. I could see lightning in the distance and sensed the eerie silence, like calm before the storm.

A bed in a Phoenix hotel was waiting for me, and by then I had guessed that I would not make it there for the night. I hoped I wouldn't miss the morning shuttle to Flagstaff city from where I would join a group on a three-day hike of the Grand Canyon.

After many hours of waiting, the flight took off in the wee hours and landed in Phoenix just as the sun was rising. I had just enough time to freshen up and catch the shuttle to Flagstaff.

At Flagstaff, I met Drew, the guide, who picked me up and four others, including a married couple from New Jersey and two sisters from Canada.

I sat in the front passenger seat next to Drew, a chatty and cheerful guide, who was deeply passionate about the Grand Canyon. I asked him if he was ever bored of being at the Grand Canyon almost every day.

'Not at all. I could live here all my life and not ever feel like I'm missing anything else,' he said with great conviction.

Drew had a practised manner in which he spoke about the Grand Canyon, the kind that comes with doing the same thing over and over again, saying the same things over and over knowing just when to pause and when to skip details to arouse curiosity in your listeners. It was rehearsed and yet it felt as though he shared all this information about the great natural wonder of the world exclusively with us.

Drew was slender with an athletic body, and not much taller than five feet and six inches. He created drama and suspense as we were driving closer to the Grand Canyon. He designed a remarkable build-up to our first view of this magnificent canyon. He relied on theatre to construct the overwhelming aura around the experience as though it needed any more selling.

'Here it is! Ta-da!' he said in a presenter's tone, as we all turned to the left. The Grand Canyon looked every bit as I had seen it in the photos and movies. He stopped the car at a viewing point, and we all got off to take in the expansive view.

The moment I stood in front of the Grand Canyon stretched out below me, I felt a strong tug at my solar plexus and my eyes welled up. It was a familiar feeling of longing, as though I had faced some loss here. At the same time, I could recognise a comforting acceptance deep within that perhaps only lifetimes of healing can bring. My subconscious was responding to something about the canyon although it was unclear about what.

Standing there, I could see the core of the earth sliced open for us to appreciate her beauty and power. This canyon vibrated at a high level while staying connected to the earth centre. My emotions perceived just a part of that connection, and my spirit responded with a mix of feelings. Those unfamiliar sensations made themselves known to me through a tug at my stomach and bringing up a pool of tears at the corner of my eyes.

It was a beautifully pure sentiment of love, peace, and beauty, all together transcending the mind's comprehension. I could only feel it, and no words would completely capture the essence of that vibration.

This first glimpse of the Grand Canyon will be my most special moment that I will always associate with the place. I believe that only going all the way there and standing at the edge of the canyon could unlock these latent energies. These are the one-of-a-kind experiences that make me continue seeking and travelling.

I was going to hike on different trails of the canyon for three days and experience its colours, raw beauty, and grandeur. The first day was the toughest of the hikes along the South Rim.

The trek company had shared instructional manuals that were thorough, down to the last detail, including the preferred fabric for t-shirts you should wear on the trek. This trip was wildly different from the treks I have completed in the East, where all one needs to do is pay up and land up. If it rains, we'll see about that. If the roads are closed, we'll see about that. If I'm not dressed right for the weather, we'll see about that. And if I lose my way, we'll see about that, too.

In Eastern cultures, so much is left to the moment; there is great surrender to the forces of nature; there is charm in not knowing and not planning too much. Most of the time you are just winging it.

In the spirit of the trek that I was to undertake in this heavily organised fashion, I followed the rules to the last line of that instruction booklet. I bought trekking shoes and broke them in; I bought socks of just the recommended thickness; I carried an extra pair of glasses and didn't wear contact lenses; I bought appropriate clothes to layer up for comfort in the weather's whimsical moods. I went by the book.

All this prep out of the way, it was time to get into the canyon and trek the stretches to experience its wild beauty from different angles and levels. I realised forty-five minutes into the trail just how out of shape I was despite my daily walks in preparation for the treks.

The trek required being able to cover steep inclines and declines on rough terrain. My daily hour of walking on flat land just didn't cut it. This was one instruction in the booklet that I didn't do much about and was struggling. The New Jersey couple and the Canadian sisters walked far ahead on a steady pace while I huffed and puffed at the switchbacks, those 180-degree turns on hiking trails that make you lose sight of how much you have covered.

I was panting, clutching my abdomen, and feeling the heat gush out of my body. It was Drew's job to stay with the stragglers in the group. In this case, it was me. He encouraged me to keep pushing, keep moving, and not stop till I get to the next switchback, and then the next.

Every time I stopped to catch a breath, the view around me—with the changing colours of the canyon as we got lower and lower down—kept me going. This was the beauty of the canyon that could only be experienced the slow and steady way, and here I was, stretching that slowness to an excruciating pace.

By the time I reached the end of the trail in front of a waterfall, the group had been waiting for me about thirty minutes, which was not too bad, I reasoned. We ate a basic lunch of sandwiches and dried nuts and fruits while Drew explained the science behind how the canyon was formed.

Geologists put the age of the Grand Canyon at 75 million years, give or take a few million years. When it comes to explaining how the canyon was formed, theories abound, including the shifting course of the Colorado River, vulcanism, continental drift, and variations in the earth's orbit. The most popular among these theories is that about 5–6 million years ago, erosion caused the Colorado River to carve through layers of volcanic rock and sediment.

I looked at the bright colours of purple, red, and magenta forming lines on the canyon's walls, and tried to imagine all of this under water a few million years ago.

A brief lunch break later, it was time to make the way back with quite many steep inclines on the way up. At one point I stopped, panting and unable to move forward anymore. The heat made me nauseated, and I didn't know if I wanted to throw up or keep going. I waited to check in with my body to see how I really felt. My discomfort was a combination of the heat, dust, and my own poor fitness level.

I mustered the courage and decided to take a step at a time in the confidence that I would not be left behind here, and that I will make it back sooner or later. My average fitness level apart, it was my mind that needed to be strong at this time. Repeating positive self-talk and affirming assurances to myself did a world of good.

Every time I gave myself a little pep talk, I walked with confidence, covering more ground faster. It was a mental game, and I had signed up to play it without knowing all the rules. In a state of desperation, I had to pull up my mental reserves and push my body to do the mind's bidding. It worked. And here was the trick to most physical routines—it started with controlling the mind.

At this point, I started a personal conversation with the Grand Canyon. The inverted mountains were testing me. They were encouraging me to push my limits. They were forcing me to be completely present here in the moment. The mountains were teaching me to meditate.

The human spirit is capable of amazing feats of strength and endurance. I was given a tiny peek into just what we could achieve only if we willed it. When my body was tired and in pain, I had to look around me at the canyons and I was infused with fresh energy. I took one step at a time, and I was able to complete the trek.

On the second day, I walked on another trail where the vegetation was starkly different from what I had seen on day one. The first day was dry and dusty in what seemed like a popular trail while this had more forest cover, greenery, and brighter colours of stones along the canyon. I did much better on this trek, perhaps I was better mentally prepared to stay on the trail for longer hours.

Over three days, I saw thousands of trekkers from all over the world intent on conquering this greatest and grandest canyon. They rafted along the Colorado River, covering the entire stretch of the canyon. They took ambitious trekking routes that covered the 14-km trek from the North Rim to the South Rim and stayed on the trail for days.

I saw young-and-fit to old and not-so-fit trekkers working their way across the canyon all with the aim of conquering their own mind, their doubts and fears, testing their ability, and their mental and physical strength. Nature is known to respond and make you more resilient, giving you the answers while facilitating the deep inner searching.

Staring at one particularly beautiful set of mesas and buttes with beautiful chasms between them, I asked Drew, 'Do these inverted mountains have names?'

'Yes. These three you see here are called Brahma, Vishnu, and Shiva,' he said instantly. Drew looked at me to see my reaction and was pleased that he had sufficiently shocked me.

'Names of Hindu Gods at the Grand Canyon? I did not expect that,' I told him, asking how they came about.

He said that he didn't know yet and would research this and let me know. I received an e-mail from Drew the day I landed in India. He had checked with an Arizona resident, also a historian and Grand Canyon enthusiast, who explained that the names of Hindu Gods were given to the most magnificent of the buttes and mesas quite by intuition based on how Charles Dutton, the earliest geologist to make a detailed record of the canyon, felt when he first saw these imposing inverted mountains that stood 5,000–6,000 feet tall.

One particular butte was so beautiful that it looked like an Oriental pagoda to Dutton, who immediately named it Vishnu's temple. He named the Hindu cluster of buttes and mesas as the 'Hindoo amphitheatre'. Dutton called the Shiva Temple a 'gigantic mass', considering it to be the 'grandest of all the buttes, and the most majestic in aspect, though not the most ornate'.

Dutton felt that Shiva's face was looking down into the dark depths of the inner abyss, quite accurately symbolising the Destroyer's ability to inspire deep introspection. Hindu God names are not the only ones gracing the canyon's buttes and mesas. Every major world culture is represented here, Drew wrote in the e-mail.

On the third day of the trek, I hiked through a trail that was again different from the first two days, passing through many flowering trees, and shades of darker reds and purples of the canyon.

A half-day trek done, I stood at a viewing point to take in my last view of the canyon for this trip. Drew asked us to not say goodbye but instead that we will meet again.

By the end of those three days, I had experienced up-close the grandeur of nature, seeing just how beautiful and miraculous she can be. At the same time, I had also understood my mind better, knowing how much I can push it, how to control it, and what tricks worked to make it go a little further. I had met the Grand Canyon for the first time, and in a way had also met, for the first time, a part of myself.

26

WAITING ON GOD IN VARANASI

Varanasi is a gateway to multiple dimensions. Heaven and earth meet at the world's oldest city—at least 3,000 years old—where Hindu believers come to die and commit their ashes to the Ganga while finding the meaning of life. It is where the cumulative dead are more in number than the living.

Sprawled on the banks of the River Ganga, at the confluence of Varuna and Asi, Varanasi is an expression of faith, hope, and a prayer to the skies.

The rising fumes from millions of funeral pyres are released to the heavens from this city, which is also called Benares or Kasi. Near the flowing waters of its holy river is the Mahasmashana or the great cremation ground, where souls leave the body to find their way to the next lifetime in another body and continue the karmic cycle of life and death. Bodies are brought here from near and far for cremation at Manikarnika Ghat.

The elements—water, wind, earth, fire, and ether—stand witness to man's deepest desires. Ascetics and monks renounce material life and find strength and inspiration in Varanasi to continue on the spiritual quest. Varanasi is also the birthplace of Yoga and Ayurveda.

Life, death, hope, and prayer converge on its eighty-four ghats—riverbanks (the highest number of riverbanks in the world)—with its steep stone steps.

Varanasi belongs to everyone and no one. Chaos and calm coexist in bardo, where spiritual aspirants meditate on the noisy ghats to ascend in their practice. On the same ghats, the devout seek a connection with their ancestors through rituals. Sanskrit chants and slokas rent the air, temple bells echo through the ghats, devotees bathe in the river, clothes are left to dry on the steps, and ashes from funeral pyres flow in the water.

The day starts and ends with *aarti*, fire veneration for the Ganga, on Dashashwamedh Ghat. In this elaborate ritual, priests dressed in uniform shiny silk robes stand on decorated platforms to make flower and food offerings to the river. They wave incense and fire to the Ganga in a choreographed ritual accompanied by the sounds of Sanskrit verse chants, loud drumbeats, and high-pitched conch shells that signal the offerings.

Every aarti is a festive affair, open for all to see and experience. Visitors from near and far gather to witness this unhinged grand celebration of faith and devotion.

Silence, reflection, and introspection emerge from the noise and apparent chaos, and herein is the magic of Varanasi. This magic is in the ripples of the river water, the echoes of temple bells, the silence of the sadhu and the reflections of the boatman who holds the oars tight, rowing down the river with practised precision. They all have one thing in common: they believe in the Ganga.

'Ganga takes care of me. She is my mother,' said Chaitanya Kumar, a twenty-four-year-old man in orange clothes from Thiruvannamalai, South India, sitting on the riverbank one morning. This monk completed his graduation in teaching and wanted to pursue his spiritual aspirations.

His guru instructed him to visit Varanasi and wait for an epiphany, a message. So, Chaitanya collected all his belongings, including two sets of clothes, a toothbrush, a pair of slippers and a towel—all of which fit inside a cloth bag—and headed for Varanasi in the train's unreserved wagon, with just enough money for a one-way ticket.

'Where do you stay? Where do you eat?' I asked him.

'I sleep here on the ghats. And someone somewhere is always kind enough to offer food. All my needs are taken care of here by Mother Ganga. I don't need anything else,' he said, visibly content. He meditated all day on the riverbanks.

'Are you close to finding the answers that you seek?' I asked him, instantly realising that it was insensitive of me to ask such a question.

But Chaitanya wasn't upset. 'I don't know yet. All I know is that I need to keep going,' he said.

I asked Chaitanya if he would be comfortable going for a walk with me. He readily agreed. We walked the narrow and winding pedestrian pathways with its complex warren of old-town alleys. At every turn and street corner sat a monk in ochre robes. At every major intersection was a street-side food stall selling hot jalebis and samosas, all-day sweet and spicy snacks.

Along the roads were the eponymously named Banarasi paan stalls, that famous mouth-freshener and digestive made with a concoction of edible rose paste, betel nuts, and flavoured seeds, all wrapped in betel leaves.

'Do you eat paan?' I asked Chaitanya Kumar. He shook his head, saying he didn't. 'Would you like to try some?' I offered. He refused.

We stopped at a food stall that was making fresh breakfast of puri served with spiced potato curry and halwa, a sweet dish made with semolina. We ate in silence, watching the goings-on on the streets.

At the end of the meal, Chaitanya struggled to finish the last bites of his puri. He smiled and said that he wasn't used to eating in the morning. 'I only eat one meal a day, around noon, and it is more than enough to keep me going all day. Today, I ate too much,' he said. I smiled back and thanked him for the company.

Early one morning, before sunrise, I took a boat ride on the river and witnessed devotion like I never had before. Believers gathered at the ghats in their hundreds to take a dip in the Ganga and wash away their sins. They would chant mantras and look to the rising sun with fervent pleas for protection and wish fulfilment.

Soap lather, discarded plastic waste, dried flowers and other unrecognisable waste floated on the water, urine and faeces mixed in it. But none of this mattered to the devout whose faith in the healing power of the Ganga transcended such petty concerns.

Men and women stepped into the river in different stages of undress and then changed into fresh clothes on the steps before visiting the temple.

That same evening, under a gloriously bright full moon of the Hindu calendar month of Karthik, the ghats lit up for Dev Diwali, the night when it is believed that the Gods descend on Earth to bathe in the Ganga. On this day, thousands of earthen oil lamps are lit along the banks of the Ganga to honour this mother-goddess, and 100,000 visitors are said to arrive at the ghats to partake of the festivities.

There was no more room to walk along the ghats, with heavy pedestrian traffic. Most of the floor space was taken up by the earthen lamps, leaving little space for pedestrians. Between 7 p.m. and 9 p.m. when people-movement was heaviest, we all had to walk slowly in a line that seemed unending and barely moving.

But in the chaos, I saw monks in deep meditation, surrounded by glowing oil lamps. Unperturbed by the loud music, chatter, and excitement, they sat still and transcended the present.

I saw families and children lighting lamps in devotion. Hordes of tourists took boat rides to capture the visual treat of a million lamps glittering on the ghats and double the number reflecting and bouncing off the water. Young boys and girls sold tea light candles with flowers in a cup made of dried leaves. Visitors bought these conveniently packaged lights and set them afloat on the river with a wish and prayer.

When the crowds thinned and the buzz reduced, when the boat rides stopped but many lights were still burning bright, I sat in the silent company of the water and lights till late into the evening. The magic of the light and devotion on display had transported me to another world, a heaven where water, fire, moonlight, and the human connection to them all are celebrated. The physical setting had enveloped me in calm and alertness. It was special to be here on this auspicious day. I savoured the moment for a long time.

Diwali, the festival of lights, urges us to get rid of the darkness within us by illuminating our inner world with the light of knowledge. As I saw the thousands of flickering lamps reflected on the river, I was carried to an ethereal world. I was connecting to the divine in me and bowing to what was within me, as it was without seeking perfection.

My breathing was calm, anchored to the atmosphere around me. I watched the grey smoke from the lamps reach the skies with the prayers of the millions of believers gathered there. I watched in silence as the minutes turned to hours when the lights started to flicker out one at a time. The thin crowds began to disperse. But the memory of that evening stayed with me. It did not matter that the river was too polluted or that the stone steps were too steep. It did not matter that it was too noisy or too chaotic. All that mattered was faith. It only mattered that we believed and were prepared to take that belief to its ultimate destination, transcending all things earthly. That night, I experienced the power of belief in all its humility.

Early the next morning, I walked past the debris of dried wicks, spilled oil, abandoned earthen lamps, and rangoli coloured powder designs on the floor. Dried leaves, flowers and used tea lights jiggled on the water surface. Devotees came again in the hundreds, pushing the debris away by sweeping the water with their arms. They took a dip and prayed with reverence.

On an elevated stone platform sat a monk dressed in all black, eyes closed in deep meditation. His right arm rested on a Yoga Danda—a thick wooden stick with a concave curve made specially to rest the arm horizontally for a long time. He suddenly opened his eyes and spoke loudly to no one in particular. It seemed like he was about to share wisdom from his meditations, so the few passers-by walked up the steps to the platform where he sat. The motley bunch prostrated before the ascetic and sat to listen.

The man spoke with great conviction about *Maya* (illusion) and the spiritual purpose of all life. He spoke about karma, action, and emotions. He spoke loudly and aggressively, like a message had shaken him out of his meditation and was asked to immediately share the learning with the world. Some men in the group asked him questions, and he replied, slightly irritated with the interruption, but still glad for the interest and attention.

Varanasi is known to host 23,000 temples, but a trip is incomplete without a visit to the famous Kashi Vishwanath Temple. I woke up at 1:30 a.m. and got dressed to catch my pre-booked autorickshaw ride to the temple. There was already a long line waiting for the temple to open for the 3 a.m. morning rituals. A limited number of visitors, based on first-come-first-serve, stand inside the sanctum sanctorum to watch the morning rituals of *abhisheka*—offerings of milk, curd, ghee, butter, sugar, fruits, turmeric, and kumkum, which are poured on the phallus-shaped manifestation of Lord Shiva.

Kashi Vishwanath Temple is a special Shiva temple as it's one of the twelve Jyotirlingas, the worship of Shiva in the form of light. It is said that one who attains a high spiritual state can see the Jyotirlinga as a column of fire piercing through the earth.

I was led by the temple volunteers to stand outside the sanctum sanctorum and although I couldn't see the ritual, I could hear the mantras and feel the energy as the cool and gentle breeze wafted across the temple complex. Once the rituals were done, the devotees were allowed to walk up to the idol and touch it, while offering a personal wish or prayer.

I followed the line and got down on my haunches to touch with both hands the idol that was installed at a lower step level on a silver carved platform. I felt a shiver of cold energy course through my body when I touched the idol. It was a magnetic force that was strong, cold, and hot at the same time.

I was aware of the waiting devotees behind me and had to quickly move out of the way. But that sensation from the stone stayed with me for a long time. I went outside the sanctum sanctorum and stood alone for a few minutes, feeling the sharpness from the stone throb and pulsate throughout my body. My heartbeat was fast and I felt slightly heady. I stood transfixed for a long time.

A priest walked up to me and asked me if I would like to offer a personal prayer for a fee. He would guide me through some rituals and then make my offering to the main idol. I agreed.

'You're not married?' he asked to confirm, as he saw that I wore no black-beaded chain nor red kumkum on my forehead, both visible signs of a married woman.

'No. Is that a problem?' I asked.

He shook his head and gestured for me sit on the floor with four others. He chanted mantras as we offered red kumkum powder, turmeric, and flowers to a smaller idol. He then took all the offerings into the main sanctum sanctorum.

A prayer is the same, made anywhere with intention, with or without props for company. I knew that this ritual may not be necessarily special, but I signed up for it any way. While travelling, I try to be open to varied experiences. I flow on the path of least resistance because we often have limited knowledge of people, cultures, and dimensions.

I have gained much by saying yes to new experiences, places, and people. This was one such. The priest had this business on the side, and I was supporting him.

I walked around the temple premises. In the dark, it looked like any other temple constructed in the mandir style popular in North India. Here was a symbol of Hinduism's resilience against foreign invasions.

This temple was destroyed during multiple Islamic incursions through history, the first recorded destruction by Qutub ud-Din Aibak in 1194 CE and the last by Aurangzeb. The invaders would demolish the temple and build a mosque over it. But every time, the temple would be rebuilt with support from merchants, wealthy devotees, and royalty. The current structure built by Queen Ahilyabai Holkar has been standing since 1780.

I went to Vishwanatha Gali, a narrow street of smaller temples, which—all at some point in history—connected to the main temple. I visited these temples, too, and walked by the shops that sold white plastic bottles holding Ganga water. The shops also sold Ganga water in metal pots that looked like copper but were not.

I turned on to the main street, still dark with an occasional scooter and autorickshaw riding past. A corner food street stall was doing brisk business, selling tea and samosas. I stopped for some tea and chatted with the stall owner. He recommended Khao Gali (eat street) for the best paan, jalebi, and fruit-flavoured yogurt drink.

I asked him about the famous Banarasi sarees, and he shared directions to a local merchant with silk at affordable prices. I thanked him and walked into the dawn for a day of food and shopping.

Varanasi was all things God and godly, but this realisation does not come at the cost of neglecting our human experience. Eat, drink, be happy while also being aware that you will have to give this all up one day at a time and place not of your choosing. In this, Varanasi is the most practical divine experience, oxymoronic as it sounds.

I have been pulled to visit Varanasi again but have also been aware that I will not be able to replicate this memorable experience. There is only one 'first time'. And there is no repeating that experience however hard we try. I want to hold on to these sensory treats from Varanasi and not override my memory with newer experiences. I have hesitated to return to Varanasi for this reason.

Or, maybe, the time is yet to come. River Ganga is yet to invite me there again. I will wait for her call.

Afterword

It was Saturday night on my first visit to the US, but all I wanted was to go to bed early and get a full night's rest. Resisting the pressure to hit the nightspots, I took a hot shower and got into comfortable pyjamas.

For the first time in my life I was sleeping on a bed with sleep number technology. I wasn't even aware till then that such mattresses existed. I lay in bed and pressed the remote to feel the mattress get firmer and soften depending on which button I pressed.

When I thought I had found my sleep number with just the right balance of back support and bounciness, I neatly arranged the pillows and prepared for an undisturbed night of blissful sleep.

The stage was set, the room was dark, the shower had washed away the day's stresses, and my head sunk into the soft pillows. But my mind was alert. I tried to adjust my sleep position, turning to the right, and then left. I slept on my stomach for a few minutes.

Then I put the pillow on my head. When nothing worked, I got up and dabbed some lavender oil on my wrist to induce sleep. I told myself that my mind was overactive all day and needed time to relax. So, I imagined walking on the beach, allowing the sounds of the waves to wash away my thoughts. It worked and I gently drifted to sleep to the imagined sound of the ocean.

I wasn't asleep for too long when a loud thud of a closing door shook me awake. It was so loud that I sat up straight thinking someone had broken into my room. I sat up groggy, but my heart was beating rapidly. I heard laughter and loud chatting in the room next door. It was a little past midnight. They must have just returned from dinner, I thought, and went back to sleep. But the noises from the room didn't stop.

I waited for a few minutes. My body was asking for rest, but my mind was awake and alert. It was now an hour since I sat up in bed and there was no sign of the chatter stopping. I could hear drinks being poured, glasses clinking, furniture moving and loud laughter. It certainly seemed like the party would carry on a while longer.

I got out of bed, drank water, stuffed cotton in my ears, and again tried to sleep. Just when I was able to shut out the noise and gradually drift into sleep, I heard a woman shout out loud. My heart leaped and I sat up in bed again disoriented and looking around to see if someone was in my room.

The woman's shrill cry sounded like she was right next to my ears. It initially felt like I had dreamt it all but when I came to my senses and realised where I was, I knew it was the party people next door. The woman was now laughing.

I sighed and looked at the clock. It was 12:30 a.m. I stared at the ceiling; my mind blank. The noises continued. So, I focused there. I heard many male voices. I started to count the different voices. There had to be three or four. I concentrated and was sure that there were four men and one woman in that room.

This was a wild party. Most of the male voices slurred. The woman sounded upbeat, speaking in a high-pitched tone. I heard the muffled sounds through the thin wall and the connecting door between the rooms. But I heard enough to know that they didn't talk about anything specific or serious. It was all small talk.

For some time there was silence. They must have finally gone to sleep, I hoped. But no. Now I heard kissing. I heard rustling, of probably bedsheets. The woman was moaning first slowly and then louder and louder.

Either she was dead drunk or her kisser was great. I heard her moans and cries for a few more minutes and decided that it was neither. She was pretending. And she didn't do a great job of it. Perhaps it didn't matter because the men were so sloshed themselves.

I listened to these scenes of debauchery unfold over the next three long hours. I was wide awake, listening in on the action. Sometime towards the middle of the night, I considered calling the lobby to complain of the loud sounds, but I didn't want to draw attention to myself. I didn't know who these people were, and I didn't even know if anything would come out of such a complaint.

The theory of probability works for a hotel room booking as it does for a train berth booking. In the former, if you're lucky, you won't have neighbours celebrating a bachelor party. In the latter, if you're lucky, you won't get a snoring passenger in your cubicle. Both are bound by time, luck, and karma.

I wasn't feeling lucky this Saturday. I suddenly heard a high-pitched hissing sound. It sounds like someone was using deodorant. I heard the woman say, 'Do you want to put some here, too?' Then I heard the hissing again and understood. It was whipped cream.

She was lying on the floor very close to the connecting door to my room. At this moment I laughed, and I hoped they heard. If they did, it didn't affect their adventures of the night, which carried on well into the wee hours when at some point I fell asleep. It was also when the woman had stopped making noises.

'Why didn't you just call the hotel lobby and complain?' my colleague Sarah asked, aghast at my ordeal of staying up all night having to listen to someone else getting action.

'I didn't want to draw any attention to myself,' I told her honestly. 'This is a foreign country, and it's my first visit here. All I know about the US is from popular media. And in your movies, I've seen how things can go wrong in split seconds. This country allows guns everywhere. People shoot if they are experiencing emotional loss, instability, rage, or if they're simply hungry, who knows?

'Maybe the hotel manager would ask the guests next door to quiet down and that could solve the matter. But there's also a chance that they are triggered in their drunkenly wild state of mind. Disturbing them in the middle of their raunchy ride wasn't going to be received well, I'd imagine. So, while the thought of complaining crossed my mind, I consciously chose not to.'

'Would you do the same if it happened in your country?' she asked.

'No. If it happened in India, I would pick up the phone and complain to the manager. These same possibilities apply to India, too. People get angry at the slightest insult on the roads. So, imagine if you're being challenged in the privacy of a hotel room. Of course, they would be angry. But I'd still complain in my country,' I told her.

I did not know how to explain why I would treat the two situations differently. When I thought through it some more, I guessed that it was the entitlement that comes with being a citizen of a country versus being just a visitor. Or could it be the fear of a lone girl 'asking for trouble'?

My colleague thought about it and agreed with my logic. Sarah said that if she were visiting India, she'd do what I did. But in the US, she would complain to the hotel.

This was not just about a foreign place or culture. I asked myself: if I had someone with me, would I still not complain? If a man were with me, would I let him call the lobby and complain? A voice in my head said yes.

There was a deathly silence in my mind for a few long and uncomfortable minutes when the realisation hit home. This was about how we behave when alone and how we behave in company. This difference is important to understand in solo travel. You cannot expect to have the same quality of experiences or do the same things as you would when alone and when travelling with people.

Every travel experience is unique. In my situation in the hotel room that night, I did what I felt was right at that moment. There was no shame in acting in the interest of self-protection while using intuition to guide my action. It would also not necessarily have been a sign of courage or independence to make a complaint if I did not feel right about it.

What mattered most was how I felt at that moment. If I complained, in all probability, the revellers would get a call from the lobby asking them to quiet down, and that would work. But there was also a chance that they would increase the decibel levels just to prove a point. In a drunken stupor with a group, anything is possible. This was not a chance I was willing to take. So, my action of inaction was right for me simply because I felt most comfortable with it.

My decision to not act to that disturbance was also an important step in understanding myself as a solo traveller. Where do I draw the line for myself? What am I willing to do, and not willing to do? These are all parameters of building my personal style as a solo traveller, eventually informing the quality of experience I wish to enjoy. Our choices, after all, shape our experiences.

Every subsequent visit to the US since this incident has been unique. With every journey, by myself, or with people, I grew in courage, strength, patience, tolerance for some things, and intolerance for some other things. I chose to do more in some situations and less in certain other situations. I fed certain values that were important to me and starved certain other values that I did not align with. This ongoing assessment has been a constant process in preparation for choosing right when at a crossroads.

These choices have eventually helped me to grow and evolve as a woman and as a traveller. The years and age, too, played a role in contributing to the maturity.

The earliest travel writing by women that I have read is a basket of biases. They seek to show off happy experiences where women are enthusiastic, laughing, discovering, curious, and taking to the road and their plates of food with a heightened sensory overload. These are but exclamation marks in the overall journey.

A lot goes on behind a woman's happy travel images. Women don't simply book travel destinations without first thinking about safety. Women don't book hotel rooms without first researching the reputation of the neighbourhood it is in. Women don't plan itineraries as per their whims and fancies.

Embracing the road is a much more challenging feat for women than it is for men who may not need to look over their shoulders when out and about. Women move differently in the world than men do. Public spaces are simply not designed equitably for all genders.

The open road means different things to a man than it does to a woman. A woman cannot take her security and personal responsibility for granted. Travelling solo is so much about what happens in the run-up to the actual journey as it is also about what eventually unfolds.

For a woman, the freedom of the road comes preloaded with her awareness of her gender, body, and sexuality. This awareness makes her time on the road a much more constrained experience than it is for men.

A journalist who interviewed me about my solo journeys once remarked, 'If everything goes well, a female solo traveller is lauded as brave and oh-so-courageous. If something goes wrong, that's the end of her.' He scoffed at the end of that sentence. He said it with some amount of bitterness, unable to understand why women needed at all to venture out of male protection.

Facing these reactions is also a part of the female solo traveller's journey. She breaks barriers and, at times, has to jump through hoops to take back her freedom and to embrace the road.

The road gets us in touch with our deepest selves, the darkest and the most compassionate part of ourselves. This is how the road enables us to heal. This part of the journey is no ha-ha-hee-hee cheerful travel. It is deep work. And to even get to do this work, women have to justify being out alone.

Solo travel for women is so much more than simply being out on the road alone. The more I am out by myself, the more parts of me I find to heal. I now realise that this is going to be a long journey. I accept the open road with arms wide open.

Seven years after the Minneapolis hotel incident, I was in a Moscow hotel room, where I faced a similar experience. I was woken up at 4 a.m. to a woman's loud moaning. I knew that this came from the corridor. I looked through the peephole and found two women engrossed in each other. I waited a few minutes, but the sounds didn't stop. So, I quickly opened the door for a split second and shut it.

The women knew that they had woken me. The sounds subsided and I went back to sleep. I saw the women at the breakfast table the next morning. They each gave me a mischievous, knowing smile. I smiled back, and everyone was happy. Even in this incident, I had chosen my action with awareness.

My evolution as a traveller does not stop with any one experience. With every step that I take out into the world, my responses to the world around me will be influenced by not just the place but also by the person that I have grown to become.

I might tire of sleepless nights in hotel rooms but will never tire of travelling.

Acknowledgements

This book has gone through quite a meandering journey of its own for the last five years, not unlike travelling through a colourful landscape, speed bumps, inclines, hairpin bends et al. It was no easy task getting these stories to your hands, dear reader.

I am indebted to a whole bunch of people—stars in their own right—who stepped in to wave the magic wand and move things along.

When I returned from my month-long sojourn in Russia in 2018, Prashant Sankaran asked me, 'What are you waiting for?' I knew what he meant. He had lit the spark for the idea that this book would become. Thank you, Prashant, for being my first reader and chief cheerleader, pushing me along pathways that I am hesitant to walk on.

Ashok Chopra has been a constant source of incredible support for my ideas, generously giving of his resources and leadership instincts to my books. Thank you.

Sonali Pawar, my editor, who has become a friend with whom I can exchange everything from weather to wellness notes. Your insights on improving the manuscript helped this book every step of the way. Thank you.

Thank you, also, to the incredibly dedicated team at Hay House India. Raghav Khattar, Nupur Hirani, and the marketing team truly own the ideas in this book as much as I do.

I thank Gulnaar Mirza, who gave her invaluable feedback and helped edit the first cut of the manuscript years ago. Thanks, Gul.

Prasad S is an editor and friend who has encouraged me every step of the way in my writing life. He calls a spade a spade and shared useful feedback on the stories. Thank you.

I thank my friend and editor, Vinay Kamat, for being the first reader of the manuscript. Thank you for being a non-judgemental witness to my writing life.

I thank fellow traveller and ace photographer Arun Bhat who continues to encourage me to travel and push the limits of my curiosity.

Priya Talwar, thank you for seeing the potential in this manuscript and for offering your advice on the structure.

Zac O'Yeah, the inspiring travel writer who has a way with words, kindly agreed to endorse my book and offer invaluable feedback. Thank you, Zac.

I would like to thank Pico Iyer for his support and encouragement during my phases of doubt and difficulty.

My friends and sisters from across the seas, Sairica Rose and Lisa Leonard, are constant sources of support. Thank you for your wisdom and presence!

Thank you, Priya Rajeesh, for helping me keep my head above the water when the going was tough.

Thank you, Joseph Philip, for helping me keep my wits about me during the testing editing and production phases.

Thank you, most importantly, to all those people I met during my travels. Some of you kept me safe. Some of you opened your hearts and minds to me. Some of you helped me open *my* mind and heart. Some of you healed me. Some of you helped me let go. Some of you left me inspired. Some of you pushed me to travel more.

Thank you to each and every one of you.

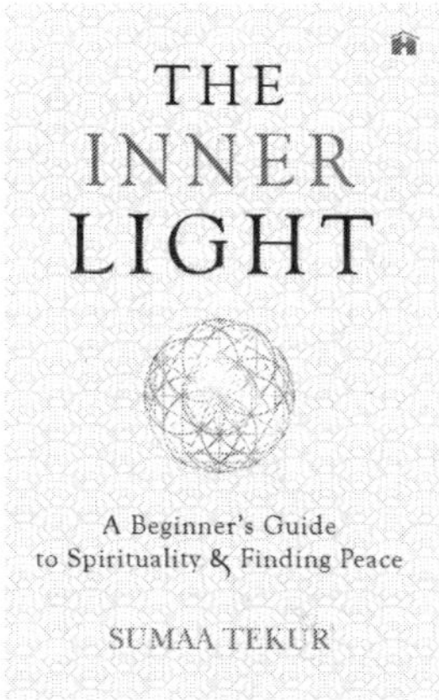

The Inner Light

The growing uncertainty of the economic climate and ever-increasing anxieties about our health and wellness have made it more urgent than ever before to seek a life of stillness, balance, and perspective. As we adjust to a new reality, our inner world is cracked open to reveal the state of our spiritual health. We are now left questioning the fragility of our egos that crumble in the face of a threat to our assumed identities of work and relationships.

The market for spirituality is an endless warren of complex pathways, with each path offering a differently worded routine to reach the same destination. Seekers are enticed with milestones to cross in the form of courses and levels often under the tutelage of a guru. This book shares wisdom on how to wade through the labyrinth of pathways that make up the journey to a more conscious spiritual lifestyle.

Rich with anecdotes from the author's own experiences and fellow seekers, *The Inner Light* is a handy guide to prepare readers—aspirants and sceptics alike—for what to expect when they set out to integrate spirituality into everyday life. This book is for beginners looking to dip their toes, and then some, into the waters of spirituality without getting caught in the whirlpool of spiritual consumerism. The book provides answers to the questions:

What is spirituality? Where do I even start?
How can I walk this path with awareness?
How can I improve my understanding of life?

Table for One

An Indian woman living alone in India is rare.

An Indian woman living alone in India by choice is rarer.

An Indian woman living alone in India by choice when her parents live in the same city is rarest.

Sumaa belongs to that rarest of breeds to join a tiny clutch of emerging single-person households in the country, ticking all those boxes—woman, single, and 'past her prime'.

This book is a reflective and an honest take on the culture and politics of an Indian woman living alone through her thirties. With her youth fading and her biological clock running out of battery, the only proposals crossing her desk are the building committee welfare bids for choice of apartment elevation, paint colour, and flowerpots next to the car park. Even there, the judgemental eyes of curious neighbours ask: 'What? There's no man in the house to make decisions?'

Rich with anecdotes, this book peels the complex layers of patriarchy, hypocrisy, and the changing social tides that leave both women and men a little more clueless by the passing day. It advocates living alone as a wholesome experience of self-discovery and for women to normalise it like marriage or living with family or roommates. While doing so, in no way does the book claim that living alone trumps co-living (okay, it actually does)!